HANDBOOK FOR HELPING OTHERS

HANDBOOK FOR HELPING OTHERS

Kenneth Stafford

Edited by Deborah D. Cole

Published by

√ chosen books
of Fleming H. Revell Company
Old Tappan, New Jersey

Library of Congress Cataloging in Publication Data
Stafford, Ken.
    Handbook for helping others.

    1. Peer counseling in the church. 2. Pastoral counseling.
I. Title.
BV4409.S83   1986   253.5   85-22546
ISBN 0-8007-9055-3

A Chosen Book
Copyright © 1986 by Ken Stafford

Chosen Books are Published by
Fleming H. Revell Company
Old Tappan, New Jersey
Printed in the United States of America

Designed by Ann Cherryman

Dedication

To my dear wife, Doreen, who has spent endless hours in prayer and in the editorial support of this book. Her personal contribution to this book—Chapter 23, "The Wife's Role"—is invaluable, making my work, as always, well-rounded.

This joint effort is to the glory of God who has revealed to us, as we have worked together, how we can be one.

Acknowledgments

I wish to acknowledge the inspiration of the Lord and the guidance of the Holy Spirit in the writing of this book.

I further extend my deep appreciation to Deborah D. Cole for the initial foundational editing. In addition, I much appreciate the excellent counsel and cooperation between this author and David Hazard, an editor-at-large for Chosen Books. The contribution of his time and talents were indispensable in bringing this book into print.

I would also like to gratefully acknowledge the following organizations and individuals for granting permission to use material:

Andelin Foundation, P.O. Box 189, Pierce City, MO 65723: *Man of Steel & Velvet* by Aubrey P. Andelin, for material on attributes of the godly husband.

Bridge Publishing, Inc., 2500 Hamilton Blvd., S. Plainfield, NJ 07080: *X-Rated Marriages* by H. Page Williams, for material on the role of godly husbands.

Christian Research Institute, Box 500, San Juan Capistrano, CA 92693: *Walter Martin's Cults Reference Bible* (Vision House Publishers, Santa Ana, Calif., 1981), for material on cults.

Dodd, Mead & Company, 79 Madison Ave., NY 10016, for quotations from *My Utmost for His Highest* by Oswald Chambers.

Dick Eastman and Change the World Ministries, 16604 Arminta Ave., Van Nuys, CA 91406:

The Hour that Changes the World by Dick Eastman (Baker Book House, Grand Rapids, Mich., 1978) for material on developing a disciplined prayer life.

Equip Ministries, Houston, Tex., for material on the spiritual protection afforded by a godly husband and father.

The Institute in Basic Youth Conflicts, Oak Brook, Ill., for material on discouragement, the basic needs of a husband and wife, and ten scriptural convictions.

Kenneth Cain Kinghorn for material of the healing of emotions, from his *Dynamic Discipleship* (Baker Book House, Grand Rapids, Mich.).

The Narramore Christian Foundation, Rosemead, CA 91770: "Assault and Battery within Wedlock," by Kim Yvonne McClintock (*Psychology for Living*, February 1983, pp. 7, 10; March 1983, pp. 8–10), for material on wife abuse.

Insight for Living, Fullerton, CA 92634: *Strike the Original Match*, a Bible study guide by Charles R. Swindoll, copyright © 1975, p. 11, all rights reserved, for five character traits of a godly father.

Tyndale House Publishers, Inc., Wheaton, IL 60189: *Spirit Controlled Temperament* by Tim LaHaye, copyright © 1966, pp. 70, 72, 83, for material on anger and fear.

Contents

SECTION IV: ONE FLESH

SECTION V: THE FAMILY

SECTION VI: THE SPIRIT OF ANTI-CHRIST

Introduction

I count it a privilege indeed to commend to you the book you now hold—and its author, my friend and co-worker Ken Stafford, a man who has enabled literally thousands of men and women to put biblical principles of counseling into practice.

During the past seven years alone, Ken has personally trained more than 10,000 Christians in crisis counseling—both for the Christian Broadcasting Network (of which he is National Training Director) and for numerous churches and ministries throughout the United States.

In so doing, the chief tool Ken has used is a version of this book, *Handbook for Helping Others*, which we at CBN now use as the standard reference in training all our counselors.

Much can be said about the great harvest of spiritual fruit that has come about through Ken Stafford and his book: the more than 1,690,000 family problems prayed for; the 36,000 potential suicides ministered to; the 500,000-plus calls for salvation answered by CBN alone since 1978. The material and approach herein have more than proved themselves in the crucible of experience.

How can we account for the remarkable effectiveness of this book? The answer lies, I think, in Ken's primary focus: not on counseling methodology (though that is not lacking), but on the nurture of each individual counselor's inner life with God through His Word. Ken's belief is that those who have received richly from God are best enabled to give freely what He has so generously bestowed upon them.

This is why I am confident that you—whether a lay person with a desire to help others, or a pastor, or a Christian counselor dealing with crisis needs—will find Ken's book a strong spur to your own spiritual growth, as well as an invaluable resource in your personal ministry to troubled people.

Pat Robertson, *President*
Christian Broadcasting Network

Preface

How many times have you desired to help someone during a time of difficulty or crisis, but felt that you were unprepared?

As you read and study the insights into God's Word brought forth in this book, you will learn some very helpful principles of biblical counseling.

You will also find your own spiritual life being enriched greatly by what you learn. And as you take time to pray for others, you will be blessed and blessed again.

No matter where you are in your walk with the Lord, you will discover that you can apply the principles herein—listening, sharing the Word, and praying with confidence—and that God's Spirit will be faithful to work through you with power as you serve others in their time of need.

Ken Stafford

I

PREREQUISITES FOR COUNSELING

The Foundation

Foundation Stones

Guiding Someone to Christ

Restoration and Reconciliation

Chapter One

THE FOUNDATION

The Christian's call to counsel comes from God Himself. It is God's desire that we aid others lovingly in solving their problems, and it is our privilege to be involved in this work. We are called to study God's Word and be available for His use.

First, we must never forget that God wants "all men to be saved and to come to the knowledge of the truth" (1 Timothy 2:4). This passage should create in the heart of every Christian the desire to bear the freeing message of Christ to all people.

Second, God includes us in His salvation process. As the New Testament says, "My brethren, if any among you strays from the truth, and one turns him back, let him know that he who turns a sinner from the error of his way will save his soul from death, and will cover a multitude of sins" (James 5:19–20).

Those who are living in error need to be corrected. We have a responsibility to share the truth with them as the Holy Spirit leads us, and this shows that we care. The apostle Paul wrote that God gave us the ministry of reconciliation. God's Word through us will restore, reconcile, and heal those who are broken and hurting. (See 2 Corinthians 5:18.)

Third, in preparing to counsel, we must absorb

the Word of God, and know that we can do all things—correct, encourage, build up—through Christ who strengthens us. (See Philippians 4:13.)

Fourth, we need to be available to God, prepared to follow His leading, and we can trust God to make us ready for His use. We must be willing to be and do whatever pleases Him. Our desire will be simply to hear Him say, "Well done, good and faithful servant."

1.1 HEART ATTITUDE

God does not desire mouthpieces who parrot His Word, but Christians who rightly apply His Word and demonstrate His nature by their actions. It is vital that the counselor develop the following heart attitudes, remembering that God is always at work in us, too.

Obedience. We must first be obedient to God's Word. Otherwise, how can we communicate it effectively to someone else? If we have sin in our lives, how can we minister to others?

As God works in our lives, He gives us something substantial to give to others. The psalmist writes, "How blessed are those who observe His testimonies, Who seek Him with all their heart" (Psalm 119:2).

If we obey God, we will walk in His ways and "do no unrighteousness" (verse 3). Certainly we fall short of this, but our heart's desire should be to seek after God continually and follow His commandments.

Our obedience and spiritual maturity will set the example and aid us as we counsel others. When another believer is overcome by a problem, we are to counsel and restore him "in a spirit of gentleness; looking to yourselves, lest you too be tempted" (Galatians 6:1).

A Servant's Heart.   Our attitude as we approach others is to be one of Christlike humility, seeking ways to serve. We are to treat others as better than ourselves, and to consider not only our personal interests but those of others. (See Philippians 2:2–4.)

It should become natural to serve others, to want the best for them and see them overcome their problems.

Jesus set the example. He came to serve others, not to be served, and in so doing He put aside His rights and became a servant.

Freedom of Spirit.   Before we can counsel, we must deal with those things in our lives that displease God. Here are Paul's words: "Since we have these promises, dear friends, let us purify ourselves from everything that contaminates body and spirit" (2 Corinthians 7:1, NIV).

Often people try to counsel others when they are struggling with a similar problem. But unless we are truly free, we are in danger of stumbling ourselves, or giving advice that is not mature. If we are still struggling, how can we give hope to another? In cases like this, it is better to refer the one seeking help to a mature Christian who does not have the same problem. And, as Solomon reminds us, there is safety in an "abundance of counselors." (See Proverbs 11:14.)

Too, our spirits can become restricted with the clutter of anger, bitterness, or resentment. We need to pray that we might be clean vessels as we seek to bring the message of hope.

Committed. Sometimes people reach out to others out of sympathy, human concern, or just wanting to help. Unless we are solidly committed to God, however, and to presenting "every man complete in Christ" (Colossians 1:28), it is too easy to hand out sympathy or homey axioms rather than the truth of God's Word.

Submissive. We are all to be subject to one another as Christians. (See Ephesians 5:21.) We need guidance in how to counsel. Being submitted to a mature Christian will give us the support we need and enable us to counsel with confidence.

We must not complain but gladly submit to every authority God has placed over us, such as our pastor and elders.

Loving. What is our attitude toward the one seeking help? Are we helping out of God's unconditional love? Human love may get discouraged and give up when the result does not come quickly, which can seriously damage the person we are counseling. But God's is a tough love that wants to see a person freed no matter what the cost or pain. It alone will endure steadfastly until freedom comes.

Too, love dictates that we not spread what we hear about the other person, which is gossip, but rather keep it in confidence among us, the counselee and God. (See 1 Corinthians 13:4–7.)

Accepting. When we love someone, we will not judge or condemn. If someone is sinning, the Holy Spirit will convict him of sin. Sometimes we may be used by God in that process, but only if our hearts are *right* not *self-righteous*.

Paul wrote, "Accept one another, just as Christ also accepted us" (Romans 15:7).

Teachable. We are never too old, too educated, or too spiritually mature to learn. We do not have all the answers to a person's problems; if we did, we would have no problems ourselves.

We learn from friends, family and others around us. Above all, God wants to teach us new insights in His Word and how to help those who come to us.

If we are not teachable, we are saying to God that we do not need Him. So it is important to recognize Jesus as our Teacher and to sit at His feet, listening to His words. (See Romans 6:17–18 and 2 Timothy 1:13–14.)

1.2 COUNSELING IN THE SPIRIT

We are not called to usurp God's role in a person's life. We are privileged to be His vessels, however, speaking His words and knowing that it is only His power that works through us to help another. In our role as vessels, we must learn to "be."

Be Open to the Work of the Holy Spirit. The only way to counsel is as the Holy Spirit leads. Our dependence, then, is on the Spirit, making counseling easier.

Jesus said He would give us "another Counselor to be with you forever—the Spirit of truth . . . you know him, for he lives with you and will be in you" (John 14:16–17, NIV).

Be Familiar with God's Word. If we do not have a scriptural base for our counseling, we should not counsel at all. We will want to share only scriptural principles or whatever will lead a person to Scripture.

Paul reminds us that "All Scripture is inspired by God and profitable for teaching, for reproof, for correction, for training in righteousness; that the man of God may be adequate, equipped for every good work" (2 Timothy 3:16–17).

God's Word is the foundation of all counseling; it is reliable in its wisdom.

Be a Listener. True listening is active. We must take time to listen to the Holy Spirit. Just as we can tune other people out, we can tune God out and not hear what He is saying.

In counseling, we need to listen not just to a person's words, but also to the heart attitude. Otherwise, our reply may be superficial or inappropriate.

Since listening is a forgotten art these days, we need to pause for a moment and consider what listening really means.

Listening takes mental effort and attention. For this reason, we must lay aside our own worries before entering a time of counseling. Since it is also important to rid ourselves of outward distractions, talking in a quiet place is helpful.

We need to give the other person time—time to collect his thoughts before speaking, time to express all that he is thinking and feeling. Even a long pause is best uninterrupted. This initial silence on our part is vital because it focuses our attention and lets the other person know that we are willing to truly listen without throwing out "ready" answers that may not get at the heart of the problem at all. In silence, we may also listen to the person's attitude and to what the Spirit may be guiding us to say.

While we are listening, we must empathize, that is, put ourselves in the other person's place as much as possible. Often this gives a clearer perspective of how he *feels*, which is as important as what he thinks.

Regardless of what a person says or how he says it, we cannot allow our emotions to enter in. We must never react in anger or irritation. That hinders openness and communicates a feeling of non-acceptance.

Although it is helpful to know ahead of time what the person wants to talk about, this is not always possible. When it is not, listening will help you to ask more probing questions that can bring the main issue into focus and to clear up any details that you may have missed or did not understand as the story unfolded.

1.3 THE GOALS OF COUNSELING

The goals of counseling are to introduce Jesus Christ and to demonstrate love and holiness, the two balancing aspects of God's nature.

Introducing Jesus Christ. Whether or not the person we counsel is a Christian, it is imperative that we introduce Jesus Christ into the situation. He is the living Savior who has the power to change a person. We need to be sure of a person's relationship and commitment to Jesus. That foundation must be solid.

We cannot change people without the power of Jesus' Spirit working in them. And, in fact, changes may not occur during the actual counseling time. But as a person gets alone with the Holy Spirit, that power begins to convict and change.

Isaiah called Jesus the "Wonderful Counselor."

(See Isaiah 9:6.) So all our counseling must be done through Him, with Him, and in Him.

The root of a person's problem is often disobedience and an inadequate knowledge of Jesus. If we are obedient and truly know Him, His love, sacrifice, and power, and His eagerness to help us, we can turn our problems over to Him. Jesus calls us to come to Him with our cares and burdens. (See Psalm 55:22.)

Love. A major aspect of God's nature is love. For this reason, we must be ready to comfort, console, and encourage when that is needed.

Without love, our counseling will be empty and legalistic. The one counseled will sense that we are doing it out of a sense of duty rather than for his good. People are hungry for the love that only God can provide. As we make ourselves available to Him, we will become channels of His love. (See 1 Corinthians 13:1–13.)

Holiness. It is also important that we be ready to demonstrate holiness, calling sin by its name and suggesting repentance, when necessary, or the severing of immoral or illegal ties.

God has called us to be holy as He is holy. (See Leviticus 20:7.) Holiness is simply being like God. And He expects us to confront sin in order to bring repentance—that is, a complete turning away from sin and turning to righteousness— which is the first step in helping a person to truly change.

The counselor's calling, then, is a high one: to confront error, sin, pain, or brokenness in the Spirit of God; comforting or confronting; and always offering the hope of Jesus Christ—a hope that is life-transforming.

Chapter 2

FOUNDATION STONES

Once we as counselors have become vessels ready for God's use, applying His Word and demonstrating His nature in our actions, we need to help the counselee move toward solving problems God's way.

2.1 SETTING A FOUNDATION

First, we must help the person to discover Jesus Christ as Savior and Lord. All change will spring from that foundation. (Please see Chapter 3 on leading someone to salvation in Christ.) A person who knows Christ personally as Savior and has made Him Lord in his life accepts salvation as a gift from God and sees himself as God's "workmanship, created in Christ Jesus for good works, which God prepared beforehand, that we should walk in them" (Ephesians 2:10).

Second, because God will not hear us if we stubbornly hold onto sin in our hearts, the counselee must confess sin to God, who will forgive him and set him free from its bondage. All sin is ultimately against God, because we are disobeying His commands to us.

But we often need to hear words of forgiveness from the lips of a flesh-and-blood human being. James encourages us to confess our sins to another person who can pray maturely for our forgiveness and release from guilt (James 5:16; see also Psalm 66:18; Isaiah 59:1–2; 1 John 1:9.)

A third prerequisite to biblical change is repentance. The counselee, after acknowledging his sin, must turn away from it and turn to righteousness.

Fourth, to do things God's way, a person must come to this desire: to please God above all else.

James exhorts us to do what God says in His Word, and not just to hear it (James 1:22). This means to obey in spite of our feelings. Such obedience is vital, for under the control of the Holy Spirit Christ enables us to do all things— including change—by His strength in us.

2.2 ACCOUNTABILITY VS. AVOIDANCE

God holds each of us accountable for our choices and actions. Human beings often want to avoid taking the responsibility for choices and actions. Sometimes we need to help a person focus on individual responsibility before he or she sees the need to change or to accept biblical solutions.

When a person has done something wrong we often ask, "Why?" But "why" questions encourage blame-shifting and avoiding confronting the problems. As a result, the counselee may never accept responsibility for his sinful action. Thus he will not find true relief from guilt.

We all need to learn the difference between disease and sin, which is the true root of many emotional and mental problems. Dr. William Glasser points out in his book *Reality Therapy* that the conventional weakness of psychology and psychiatry is that morality has been left out.

The Bible, on the other hand, the only true book of preventive psychology ever written, teaches that sin is not natural to man and that we choose to sin by our own will.

God created man in His image to be like Him, without sin. Whenever man chooses to sin by his own free will, he rebels against God's purpose for his life and reaps the consequences of his act: separation from his Creator. In this act, God holds a man totally accountable. (See Romans 6:23.)

Yet the Bible teaches that man can and must resolve his sin through Jesus Christ. And it reveals that Jesus paid the price for all our sins when He died on the cross.

Charles Finney once said it was the job of the Christian worker to take sides with God against sin and to tear down all the sinner's hiding places. This we can do by helping a person understand that Jesus Christ frees us from all sin and enables us to live a guilt-free life. This is possible only when we accept personal accountability and re-sponsibility for our lives and deal with sin God's way.

We can encourage the counselee to accept personal accountability and responsibility for his problems by asking "what" questions—questions that uncover and face sin head-on. The following questions will help the counselee dig for answers, thus pointing him to accountability:

What is your problem? (Look for root causes here, such as attitudes, and be sure to listen to both the person and the Holy Spirit.)

What have you done about it?

What do you want me to do?

What motivated you to seek help?

Is there something else related to this problem that I should know?

2.3 OFFERING HOPE

Sometimes in counseling we may need to give someone reasons for hoping he can change. Several of these follow.

First, God forgives and forgets our sin. As the New Testament writer quotes Him, "And their sins and their lawless deeds I will remember no more" (Hebrews 10:17).

Second, God designs circumstances for our good, in that He "causes all things to work together for good to those who love God, to those who are called according to His purpose" (Romans 8:28).

Third, God promises a way to solve any problem and the ability to overcome any difficulty. Paul confirms this:

"No temptation has overtaken you but such as is common to man; and God is faithful, who will not allow you to be tempted beyond what you are able, but with the temptation will provide the way of escape also, that you may be able to endure it" (1 Corinthians 10:13).

2.4 BIBLICAL RENEWAL

The Bible establishes a definite pattern for change: First, we lay aside the old self, ceasing to do things our way; second, we begin to renew our mind, adopting God's perspective; and third, we put on the new self, doing things God's way. (See Ephesians 4:22–24.)

There are several steps a person should take to bring about change.

First, he should identify those sins in his life that separate him from a close relationship with God or with other people. These could include anger, lying, adultery, drug abuse, and other acts of rebellion.

Then he needs to identify those attitudes or actions that will allow him to be more like Christ, such as the fruit of the Spirit. (See Galatians 5:22–23.)

He also needs to recognize the barriers— selfishness, pride, fear, and the like—that hinder his putting off the old self and putting on the new self.

Next, a person needs to identify those factors, like links in a chain, that contribute to his choosing to sin. He may need to remove himself from the company of those who do not know and follow God's principles, until he solves his problems and has established a biblical pattern of doing things. And he will want to seek help from others who are spiritually mature, firmly grounded in God's Word and living godly lives.

To establish a program for renewing the mind, see Section II, Toward Spiritual Maturity.

2.5 OBEDIENCE

The road to change is paved by practicing obedience daily. Change is a process. Just as a baby learns to walk one step at a time, so we learn to walk in God's way one step at a time. We are to walk wisely, learning to be faithful in the very little things God asks us to do, and then in the greater things.

We must discipline ourselves, never growing weary of doing what God wants us to do. In due time we will see the results of that discipline. Obedience will have become an established pattern, a habit.

As counselors, we must never be discouraged by temporary failures. We can encourage the counselee to confess those failures to God and repent, finding forgiveness and righteousness. Since failures can be the result of hidden or unknown sin, examining oneself and asking the Holy Spirit to reveal unknown sin may also be necessary for biblical change.

As the pattern of confession and true repentance is established, a person will rise up and begin again to live the life of freedom and wholeness that God has planned for him, knowing he is training his senses to discern good and evil. (See 1 John 1:9; Hebrews 5:14; Acts 26:20.)

Chapter 3

GUIDING SOMEONE TO CHRIST

We have established that a person needs to make a personal commitment to Jesus Christ, and to know Him as Lord and Savior before he can solve problems biblically. It is important to determine, then, just where a person stands in his relationship with God.

Sometimes the worst thing to ask is, "Are you saved?" You may prefer to ask, "Who is Jesus to you?" or, "What does Jesus mean to you personally?" or, "What is your relationship to Jesus Christ?"

If the counselee indicates he knows Jesus Christ, ask him to be more specific about when and where he made the commitment. If the person avoids answering the question, you might ask, "What will happen to you when you die?"

3.1 SALVATION AND THE WORD

There are certain principles to consider in guiding someone to salvation in Christ.

Salvation is urgent. An accident may take the life of someone precious to us, or even our own life. We do not know what will happen from one day to the next. Now is the time to make a commitment, as the apostle wrote: "Behold, now is 'the day of salvation'" (2 Corinthians 6:2).

Salvation is God's will. We established at the outset that God desires every person in the world to be saved and to come to a knowledge of the truth. (See 1 Timothy 2:4.) He loves us all and sent Jesus, His Son, to be the payment for our sins so that we could be saved. There is only one way to God, moreover, and that way is Jesus. Jesus Himself said, "I am the way, and the truth, and the life; no one comes to the Father, but through Me" (John 14:6).

Mankind needs a Savior, someone who will pay for his sin. "The wages of sin is death," Paul wrote, "but the free gift of God is eternal life in Christ Jesus our Lord" (Romans 6:23).

Because sin had to be paid for through death, Jesus came to earth to pay for our sin through His own death. Jesus had to die in order to give us eternal life. (See Matthew 20:28 and Hebrews 9:22.)

We did nothing to merit this free gift. In fact, God the Father showed us His love by sending Jesus to die for us "while we were yet sinners." (See Romans 5:8.) Only the shed blood of Jesus reconciles us to God and makes a way for us to have a relationship with God.

Again Paul wrote to the Romans: "Much more then, having now been justified by His blood, we shall be saved from the wrath of God through Him. For if while we were enemies, we were reconciled to God through the death of His Son, much more, having been reconciled, we shall be saved by His life" (Romans 5:9–10; see also 2 Corinthians 5:21).

Being born again spiritually—having a new birth—transfers us from darkness, under Satan's rulership, to light, where God rules. (See Colossians 1:13.)

HANDBOOK FOR HELPING OTHERS

In Satan's kingdom of darkness, a person lacks direction, becomes anxious over problems, is confused about life, and experiences broken relationships. But in God's Kingdom of light a person has purpose and hope, maintains inner peace, achieves true happiness, and has healthy relationships with others. Godly relationships are pure, right, and holy in His sight—loving relationships that are not manipulative, abusive, or demanding.

This Kingdom of light is available now to the one who believes. (See Colossians 1:13.)

3.2 THE COST

Giving one's life to Christ requires more than a one-time decision; it demands commitment. What is really asked of one who desires to follow Christ? In anyone who truly wants to begin a Christian life, we must try to cultivate the following attitudes.

Seeking. To seek after God means to search for Him, to long for His companionship and His presence. He has promised to let us find Him if we search for Him with all our heart. (See Jeremiah 29:13.)

He has also promised that "those who hunger and thirst for righteousness" are blessed and shall be satisfied. (See Matthew 5:6.)

Honest. The one who desires to make a commitment to Christ must have an honest, upright heart. As Jesus explained in the Parable of the Sower: "And the seed in the good ground, these are the ones who have heard the word in an honest and good heart, and hold it fast, and bear fruit with perseverance" (Luke 8:15).

Brokenhearted. We must develop a contrite or broken heart before God, willing to yield ourselves totally to Him and giving up our own desires for His. With a broken and contrite heart, we know God is near us. (See Psalm 34:18 and Psalm 51.)

Submissive. Just as servants are to be submissive to their masters with all respect, so are we to be submissive to God's authority over our lives, willing to be led by Him. And we are to respect Him at the same time. (See 1 Peter 2:18 and Mark 10:15.)

Repentant. We must be repentant or willing to change, ready to acknowledge our ways as sinful and turn from them to doing things God's way. (See Luke 5:32.)

Committed. The one who commits his life to Christ is willing to die to his own desires and forsake everything.

Jesus offered this formidable challenge: "If anyone comes to Me, and does not hate his own father and mother and wife and children and brothers and sisters, yes, and even his own life, he cannot be My disciple" (Luke 14:26; see also John 12:24–25 and Luke 18:22–23.)

3.3 QUESTIONS LEADING TO SALVATION

To the person who desires salvation, the following two questions may be helpful.

Are you willing to stop going your own way and begin to live God's way, by asking Jesus Christ to be the Lord of your life?

The apostle Paul described what it means to die to our selfish ways: "I have been crucified with

Christ; and it is no longer I who live, but Christ lives in me; and the life which I now live in the flesh I live by faith in the Son of God, who loved me, and delivered Himself up for me" (Galatians 2:20).

Are you ready to confess before others that Jesus Christ is your Lord?

Public confession is necessary for salvation, as Paul wrote to the Romans: "If you confess with your mouth Jesus as Lord, and believe in your heart that God raised Him from the dead, you shall be saved; for with the heart man believes, resulting in righteousness, and with the mouth he confesses, resulting in salvation" (Romans 10:9–10).

3.4 PRAYER

After being assured that a person wants to commit his or her life to Christ, offer to join in prayer to make that commitment. You will want to include the following elements in your prayer.

Simple Belief in Jesus Christ as God's Son. A familiar verse affirms this: "For God so loved the world, that He gave His only begotten Son, that whoever believes in Him should not perish, but have eternal life" (John 3:16).

And later in the New Testament we find, "These things I have written to you who believe in the name of the Son of God, in order that you may know that you have eternal life" (1 John 5:13).

Confession. As we mentioned earlier, the person must confess publicly that Jesus is Lord of his life. We have the promise "that every tongue should confess that Jesus Christ is Lord, to the glory of God the Father" (Philippians 2:11).

Public confession will help seal and solidify one's commitment to follow Jesus.

Forgiveness. All sin is ultimately against God. Therefore, the person must ask God to forgive him.

The psalmist David wrote, "Wash me thoroughly from my iniquity, and cleanse me from my sin. . . . Against Thee, Thee only, I have sinned, And done what is evil in Thy sight" (Psalm 51:2, 4; see also Luke 11:4 and Isaiah 1:18).

Forgiveness also involves asking for pardon from those we have offended. (See Matthew 5:23–24.)

Repentance. [Jesus Christ] did not "come to call righteous men but sinners to repentance" (Luke 5:32). This, then, is a key element in committing one's life to Him, in turning from going one's own way to obeying God.

Jesus also warned that "unless you repent, you will all likewise perish" (Luke 13:3).

It is God's kindness that leads us to repentance. He knows repentance is for our good, to bring us into a full, healthy relationship with Him and with others. (See Romans 2:4 and 2 Peter 3:9.)

And repentance is not just a one-time event. It goes beyond being sorry; it involves change. We should walk in a repentant spirit daily, which speaks of humility and brokenness. (See Luke 9:23 and 24:47.)

Commitment to Christ. As a person entrusts his life to Christ, asking Him to be in charge of everything, his thoughts and plans will become ordered and established. He will acquire a new way of looking at things. And a sure and certain peace will grow in his heart. (See Proverbs 16:3.)

No prayer or formula can truly lead a person to Christ. We must depend only on the gospel of Jesus Christ and the work of the Holy Spirit. But it may help to use the following prayer as a guide in praying with someone to make a commitment:

"Dear Lord Jesus, forgive me of my sins. I take You at Your Word that You forgive those who ask. I believe that You died for me, were buried and rose on the third day, and now sit at the right hand of the Father. I ask You to be my Lord, as You are my Savior. I give myself to You. Thank You for being faithful, for forgiving me of my sins, and for saving me. I have asked and believe that You have saved me. Amen."

3.5 GUIDELINES FOR NEW CHRISTIANS

We ought to encourage a new Christian in several pursuits.

Study God's Word. Paul encourages Christians to "Be diligent to present yourself approved to God as a workman who does not need to be ashamed, handling accurately the word of truth" (2 Timothy 2:15).

Encourage a new Christian to begin studying the easy-to-understand books of the Bible, such as the four Gospels.

Pray without Ceasing. Prayer is two-way conversation with God. It involves both talking and listening to Him. He is always there, always waiting for us to come to Him with our praise and petitions. Prayer satisfies a need inside us to express all our thoughts and feelings, all the deepest longings within us. And God alone is able and willing to meet those needs and satisfy those longings.

The apostle Paul exhorted us to have a productive prayer life, to maintain an attitude of prayer at all times, to be able to pray spontaneously as any need arises. (See 1 Thessalonians 5:17.)

Fellowship with Believers. Paul gives us an example of fellowship among the New Testament believers:

"And they were continually devoting themselves to the apostles' teaching and to fellowship, to the breaking of bread and to prayer. And day by day continuing with one mind in the temple, and breaking bread from house to house, they were taking their meals together with gladness and sincerity of heart, praising God, and having favor with all the people" (Acts 2:42, 46–47).

Exercise Faith. Just as muscles must be exercised to stay healthy and useful, our faith must be exercised, too. Whenever an opportunity comes up for trusting God, we can encourage the new Christian to stretch his faith, no matter how great or how small that opportunity may seem.

The brother of our Lord wrote that "faith, if it has no works, is dead, being by itself" (James 2:17).

One further and very important note: While Christians are sometimes divided on the subject of water baptism and its role in the spiritual growth of the new believer, we must encourage the new believer in Christ at least to view water baptism as an outward sign of an inward reality—the circumcision of the heart. (See Colossians 2:11–12.)

Paul was quite clear that "we have been buried with [Christ] through baptism into death, in order that as Christ was raised from the dead through the glory of the Father, so we too might walk in the newness of life. For if we have become united with Him in the likeness of His death, certainly we shall be also in the likeness of His resurrection" (Romans 6:4–5).

Many counselors have discovered, too, that failure on the part of Christians to be obedient in the area of water baptism has sometimes revealed a broader attitude of disobedience inwardly. Any such disobedience can mean that one will always be stunted in spiritual growth.

3.6 BENEFITS FOR NEW CHRISTIANS

The new Christian will derive many benefits from his new life in Christ. We can further strengthen the new believer by helping him to understand his heritage in Christ.

First, he becomes a child of God. According to the apostle John, "But as many as received Him, to them He gave the right to become children of God, even to those who believe in His name" (John 1:12).

As a child of God, he becomes an heir of God and a fellow heir with Christ. (See Romans 8:16–17 and Galatians 3:26.)

Second, he becomes a new creation. One of the most wonderful promises for a Christian is that his old sin nature and all the things he did before he committed his life to Christ have passed away. He is a "new creature"; every single thing in his life has become new.

His slate is clean because the blood of Jesus

Christ has cleansed him from all his sin. He makes a brand-new start in life, for God remembers his sin "no more" (Jeremiah 31:34; see also Galatians 6:15 and Ephesians 2:10).

Third, he shares in God's divine nature. That is, he actually has God's nature residing in him, enabling him to choose God's way.

The Bible says, "[God's] divine power has granted to us everything pertaining to life and godliness. . . . For by these He has granted to us His precious and magnificent promises, in order that by them you might become partakers of the divine nature" (2 Peter 1:3-4).

Fourth, this new believer shares in his own experience Christ's victory over sin and the world, according to his measure of faith.

In John's first epistle, we see that "whatever is born of God overcomes the world; and this is the victory that has overcome the world—our faith. We know that no one who is born of God sins; but He who was born of God keeps him and the evil one does not touch him" (1 John 5:4, 18).

The new Christian also has an exciting promise to carry with him wherever he goes: "You are from God, little children, and have overcome [the wickedness of the world]; because greater is He who is in you than he who is in the world" (1 John 4:4).

Chapter 4

RESTORATION AND RECONCILIATION

We who have sinned and broken our fellowship with God need to be restored to a whole relationship with Him. And again, God has made a way—reconciliation.

Achieving reconciliation involves several steps. God must first convict the sinner. A person may be doing many "good" things, but God sees his heart. Jesus warned the Christians at Ephesus, "But I have this against you, that you have left your first love" (Revelation 2:4). God can use any means to point out sin, but when He convicts through the Holy Spirit, it is constructive. When a person is open to Him, he or she will heed the conviction and repent.

Sometimes God uses us to speak to the sinner, since He has given to us the work of reconciling others to Him. As Paul wrote, "God, who reconciled us to Himself through Christ, and gave us the ministry of reconciliation, namely, that God was in Christ reconciling the world to Himself, not counting their trespasses against them, and He has committed to us the word of reconciliation" (2 Corinthians 5:18–19).

As a conciliator and restorer, you may bring God's word of conviction and reconciliation to the one who has sinned. And through the conviction of the Holy Spirit, that one will desire to return to his God. His prayer will be as the psalmist's: "Create in me a clean heart, O God, and renew a steadfast spirit within me" (Psalm 51:10).

The person with such a desire for God will ask God's Spirit to search his heart and see if there is any sin in him. (See Psalm 139:23–24.) And, humbling himself before God, he will seek to be restored to a right relationship with Him, in which God's presence is real to him and God's love allowed to flow freely through him.

To such a repentant searcher God promises, "Therefore if any man is in Christ, he is a new creature; the old things passed away; behold, new things have come" (2 Corinthians 5:17).

We may give assurance to that person that friendship with God is renewed, and reconciliation is complete.

II

TOWARD SPIRITUAL MATURITY

A New Perspective

Baptism in the Holy Spirit

Handling "Rights"

Finding God's Will

Prayer and Fasting

Trials and Suffering

Developing Godly Attitudes
and Character

Healing

Principles of Giving

Chapter 5

A NEW PERSPECTIVE

Man consists of three parts: spirit, soul and body. Our spirit is the part of us that unites with Christ when we accept Him into our lives. It is the eye, the heart, the center of our being. It is the part of us that comes into contact with Him immediately when we say, "Come into my heart, Lord Jesus. I accept You as my Lord and Savior."

When you make that kind of commitment, believing in your heart, then your spirit and God's Spirit unite and you become one. If you have made a genuine commitment to Christ, then nothing can break that union. God has promised in His Word that nothing can separate us from His love. (See Romans 8:38–39.)

The next part of our being is the soul or psyche. This includes the mind, the will, and the emotions. When we are controlled solely by our human soul, pleasing self is more important than pleasing God. (See John 3:6.)

A Christian who desires to please God, of course, may still stumble into sin. But a person who has life-dominating sins needs to learn to walk after the Spirit and not after his fleshly desires or his soul. (See Romans 8:6.)

Only one kind of Christian exists—the one who desires to follow Jesus Christ, not his flesh. The natural man, or one who has not made a commitment to Christ, lives in rebellion against God, with no knowledge of truth.

As a person's spirit unites with Jesus Christ and he yields to the work of the Holy Spirit, he matures and grows. As a result, the fruit of the Spirit is produced in his life. (See Galatians 5:22–23.) The Holy Spirit radiates from the spirit to the soul—mind, will, and emotions—and out through the body. This is the process of sanctification, in which we are conformed to the image of Christ. (See Romans 12:1–2.) As we allow Him to take over our lives, we will slowly grow more "numb" to the pulls of the flesh, and grow stronger in the power of Christ.

This section is intended to help the believer who truly wants to come to the end of selfish, soulish desires and begin to walk in the Spirit of the living God.

Chapter 6

BAPTISM IN THE HOLY SPIRIT

Many questions have been raised on the subject of the baptism in the Holy Spirit. Let's look to the Bible for the answers.

6.1 WHO IS THE HOLY SPIRIT?

The Holy Spirit, the Spirit of God, is God's gift and promise to us. Jesus said He would "ask the Father, and He will give you another Helper, that He may be with you forever" (John 14:16).

Jesus promised that the Holy Spirit would come to His followers after He had ascended to the Father. He would send Him as a Comforter who would come upon them. The Holy Spirit would also empower and guide them to the truth. He would not leave them alone.

The Holy Spirit is our source of power and love. (See John 15:26; 16:7; Acts 1:4–5; Romans 5:5.)

6.2 WHO CAN RECEIVE THE BAPTISM IN THE HOLY SPIRIT?

The baptism in the Holy Spirit is available to all born-again believers.

In Acts 19:2–6 Luke records the following conversation between Paul and some disciples:

"And he said to them, 'Did you receive the Holy Spirit when you believed?' And they said to him, 'No, we have not even heard whether there is a Holy Spirit.' And he said, 'Into what then were you baptized?' And they said, 'Into John's baptism.' And Paul said, 'John baptized with the baptism of repentance, telling the people to believe in Him who was coming after him, that is, in Jesus.' And when they heard this, they were baptized in the name of the Lord Jesus. And when Paul had laid his hands upon them, the Holy Spirit came on them, and they began speaking with tongues and prophesying." (See also John 3:3–6; Acts 2:38; Acts 8:12–17.)

6.3 WHY DO CHRISTIANS NEED THE BAPTISM IN THE HOLY SPIRIT?

In Ephesians 5:18 Paul commanded believers to be filled with the Spirit. It is a command for all believers, not just for some. Being filled, or baptized, with the Holy Spirit is a simple act of obedience to God's Word.

Just before Jesus' ascension to the Father, He gathered His disciples together, commanding them "not to leave Jerusalem, but to wait for what the Father had promised, which" He said, "you heard of from Me; for, John baptized with water, but you shall be baptized with the Holy Spirit not many days from now" (Acts 1:4–5).

Until we are filled with the Holy Spirit, we do not have power to live the Christian life or to love others. Jesus told His disciples that when the Holy Spirit came upon them, they would receive power to be His witnesses throughout the whole world. (See Acts 1:8.)

The power and love produced in one's life by receiving the infilling of the Holy Spirit becomes a powerful witness to those who have not made Jesus Lord of their lives.

6.4 WHO IS THE BAPTIZER?

The Lord Jesus Christ baptizes believers with the Holy Spirit—a truth brought out in each of the four Gospels. John the Baptist made the emphatic declaration: "As for me, I baptize you in water for repentance, but He who is coming after me is mightier than I, and I am not even fit to remove His sandals; He Himself will baptize you with the Holy Spirit and fire" (Matthew 3:11; see also Mark 1:7–8; Luke 3:16; John 1:33).

When a person receives the baptism in the Holy Spirit, he says to God, "I want all of You. And I want You to have all of me. I want to go deeper in my knowledge of and relationship with You."

So being filled with the Spirit is not a one-time experience; rather, it must occur daily. We need a constant infilling of power and love.

Who among us would be satisfied just to be a believer without having all God wants us to have?

6.5 HOW DO WE RECEIVE THE BAPTISM IN THE HOLY SPIRIT?

Jesus said, "If any man is thirsty, let him come to Me and drink. He who believes in Me, as the Scripture said, 'From his innermost being shall flow rivers of living water'" (John 7:37–38).

First, we must be acutely aware of our need for spiritual water. Many do not drink from the fountain of living water because they are satisfied with their condition and have no desire for a deeper walk with God. (See John 4:10.)

Next, we are to seek the Giver, not the gift. Too

often when we seek to be filled with the Holy Spirit, we seek the outward evidence of the gift. Jesus, who gives us the gifts through His Holy Spirit, wants us to look to Him and Him alone.

Third, we must prepare our hearts. Unresolved sin will hinder our being filled with the Holy Spirit. How can He move into our lives when bitterness or unforgiveness or some other life-dominating sin blocks the way? We must confess our sin and repent of it in order to receive His Holy Spirit.

Fourth, we can relax and believe God to act. Filling us with the Holy Spirit is His work, not ours. We have only to enter our prayer closet and receive by faith by asking Him to fill us; then wait on Him.

"If you then, being evil, know how to give good gifts to your children, how much more shall your heavenly Father give the Holy Spirit to those who ask Him?" (Luke 11:13; see also James 4:10).

We also read in Acts 11:15–17: "And as I [Peter] began to speak, the Holy Spirit fell upon them, just as He did upon us at the beginning. And I remembered the word of the Lord, how He used to say, 'John baptized with water, but you shall be baptized with the Holy Spirit.' If God therefore gave to them the same gift as He gave to us also after believing in the Lord Jesus Christ, who was I that I could stand in God's way?"

Fifth, we must yield ourselves to God to praise and worship Him with our tongues; and, as Jesus promised, from our "innermost being shall flow rivers of living water" (John 7:38).

In Acts 10:44–46 we see: "The Holy Spirit fell upon all those who were listening to the message. And all the circumcised believers who had come with Peter were amazed, because the gift of the Holy Spirit had been poured out upon the Gentiles also. For they were hearing them speaking with tongues and exalting God."

6.6 WHAT ARE THE EVIDENCES OF THE BAPTISM IN THE HOLY SPIRIT?

1 Corinthians 12 and 14 call for careful study to understand how the Holy Spirit makes Himself known in the life of the believer. These chapters list some of the gifts of the Spirit.

As Paul wrote, "There are varieties of gifts, but the same Spirit. But to each one is given the manifestation of the Spirit for the common good. But one and the same Spirit works all these things, distributing to each one individually just as He wills" (1 Corinthians 12:4, 7, 11).

In the Gospel of John, Jesus tells us more about the Holy Spirit's role in our lives: "But the Helper, the Holy Spirit, whom the Father will send in My name, He will teach you all things, and bring to your remembrance all that I said to you" (John 14:26).

It is in the Holy Spirit's role as Helper, which in the Greek *(Paracletos)* means one who is called alongside, that we see Him manifested most clearly. We can look for evidences of this Helper, therefore, at work in our own lives.

Power. The Holy Spirit fills us with power to overcome sin and to be effective witnesses of Christ's life, death, and resurrection.

Just before ascending to the Father, Jesus told His disciples that He was "sending forth the promise of My Father upon you; but you are to stay in the city until you are clothed with power from on high" (Luke 24:49).

Also, according to Luke, Jesus promised: "but you shall receive power when the Holy Spirit has come upon you; and you shall be My witnesses both in Jerusalem, and in all Judea and Samaria, and even to the remotest part of the earth" (Acts 1:8).

Tongues. Releasing one's tongue to the Lord is probably one of the most difficult requests our Lord asks of us. But by our desire to control it, we actually manifest rebellion towards God's Word.

Why is it so important for us to yield our tongue to Him?

In James 3, we are reminded how unruly our tongue is. By blessing and cursing with our mouth, we prove how undisciplined we are in our relationship with God.

Our Lord wants every part of us, which means we must release that last holdout, our tongue, to Him. It is through this release that we glorify our Lord with His gift of a new heavenly language, which according to the Scriptures edifies us and which only He understands.

Out of this release, we can be assured that we have indeed been filled with His Holy Spirit, just as the first-century Christians were.

On the day of Pentecost, the Holy Spirit filled the disciples present in the Upper Room, who "began to speak with other tongues, as the Spirit was giving them utterance" (Acts 2:4).

Other Scripture passages record speaking in tongues as evidence of the Holy Spirit's presence in a believer's life. In the book of Acts, Jewish believers were amazed that "the gift of the Holy Spirit had been poured out upon the Gentiles also. For they were hearing them speaking with tongues and exalting God" (Acts 10:45–46).

Later the apostle Paul laid his hands on other believers and "the Holy Spirit came on them, and they began speaking with tongues and prophesying" (Acts 19:6).

Among Jesus' last words to His disciples was this promise: "And these signs will accompany those who have believed: in My name they will cast out demons, they will speak with new tongues" (Mark 16:17).

Being filled with the Holy Spirit and speaking in tongues has several important benefits for the believer.

Praying in tongues, as Paul says, cleanses us and frees the Holy Spirit to work in our lives: "Therefore, having these promises, beloved, let us cleanse ourselves from all defilement of flesh and spirit, perfecting holiness in the fear of God" (2 Corinthians 7:1).

We learn to enter into intercessory prayer, travailing in our souls for people and circumstances. "The Spirit also helps our weakness; for we do not know how to pray as we should, but the Spirit Himself intercedes for us with groanings too deep for words" (Romans 8:26).

Praying in tongues exercises our spirit and therefore edifies us. Jude 20 tell us, "But you, beloved, building yourselves up on your most holy faith; praying in the Holy Spirit."

Praying in tongues frees us to praise and worship God in a language only He can understand. And we know from Scripture that God is enthroned upon our praises.

We are also better able to resist the enemy when we allow God to inhabit our praises and our lives. Praying in tongues then becomes a spiritual weapon against the enemy.

"For we are the true circumcision," Paul wrote, "who worship in the Spirit of God and glory in Christ Jesus and put no confidence in the flesh" (Philippians 3:3).

Healing. The Holy Spirit makes Himself known in a believer through healing. (See 1 Corinthians 12:9.)

After being filled with the Holy Spirit, for example, Peter and John were used by God to bring healing to the lame beggar at the gate of the Temple. (See Acts 3:1–10.)

For more complete instruction on healing, please see Chapter 12.

Love. The baptism in the Holy Spirit is a baptism of love in the heart of the believer. According to Romans 5:5, "the love of God has been poured out within our hearts through the Holy Spirit who was given to us."

In His role as Helper, the Holy Spirit helps us to love other people, even the unlovely. He helps us to love ourselves and, most of all, God.

Paul exhorts us to love, assuring us that love is even more important than speaking in a heavenly tongue: "If I speak with the tongues of men and of angels, but do not have love, I have become a noisy gong or a clanging cymbal" (1 Corinthians 13:1).

Power, Love, and a Sound Mind. The Bible says that God has not given us a spirit of fear. (See 2 Timothy 1:7.) Power and love and a sound mind (in some places translated *self-control* or *discipline*) are possible through the presence of the Holy Spirit.

Direction. In His role as guide, the Holy Spirit directs us in God's ways. But we must set our minds on spiritual desires and goals.

"For those who are according to the flesh set their minds on the things of the flesh, but those who are according to the Spirit, the things of the Spirit. For the mind set on the flesh is death, but the mind set on the Spirit is life and peace. For all who are being led by the Spirit of God, these are sons of God"(Romans 8:5–6, 14).

Help in Weakness. The Holy Spirit helps us in our weakness, whether to overcome temptation or to pray as we should. (See Romans 8:26.)

Fruit. A tree that has been cared for properly with enough water, good food, and light will bear fruit. That fruit is evidence of the care.

A believer who is filled with the Holy Spirit will bear fruit. That fruit is evidence of the Spirit's presence in his life and of his right relationship with God.

This spiritual fruit, as we have already noted, is "love, joy, peace, patience, kindness, goodness, faithfulness, gentleness, self-control" (Galatians 5:22–23).

Truth. Jesus spoke clearly of the Holy Spirit's role as guide in the believer's life: "But when He, the Spirit of truth, comes, He will guide you into all the truth; for He will not speak on His own initiative, but whatever He hears, He will speak; and He will disclose to you what is to come" (John 16:13).

The Holy Spirit teaches us all things and reminds us of all that Jesus has said to us in the Bible. (See John 14:26.)

Righteousness, Peace, and Joy. As Paul wrote to the Roman Christians, "The kingdom of God is not eating and drinking, but righteousness and peace and joy in the Holy Spirit" (Romans 14:17).

Boldness. The Holy Spirit gives the believer boldness to speak forth the gospel of Jesus Christ. In Acts we read that "when [the disciples] had prayed, the place where they had gathered together was shaken, and they were all filled with the Holy Spirit, and began to speak the word of God with boldness" (Acts 4:31).

Life and Peace. Jesus said, "It is the Spirit who gives life; the flesh profits nothing; the words that I have spoken to you are spirit and are life" (John 6:63).

And in Romans 8:6 we see that "the mind set on the flesh is death, but the mind set on the Spirit is life and peace."

Worship and Praise. The believer who is filled with the Holy Spirit will also be filled with worship and praise to God the Father.

Jesus told the Samaritan woman, "the true worshipers shall worship the Father in spirit and truth; for such people the Father seeks to be His worshipers. God is spirit; and those who worship Him must worship in spirit and truth" (John 4:23–24).

Prayer and Singing. Praying and singing with one's spirit becomes possible through the baptism in the Holy Spirit. "I shall pray with the spirit," Paul said, "and I shall pray with the mind also; I shall sing with the spirit and I shall sing with the mind also" (1 Corinthians 14:15).

Casting Out Demons. Jesus said, "These signs will accompany those who have believed: in My name they will cast out demons" (Mark 16:17).

For more complete instruction on demons, please see Chapter 33.

One Body. "For by one Spirit we were all baptized into one body, whether Jews or Greeks, whether slaves or free, and we were all made to drink of one Spirit" (1 Corinthians 12:13). The Holy Spirit baptizes us into one Body with all other believers. We become members of that one Body.

Overcoming. With the power of the Holy Spirit, the believer can overcome the influence of the world upon his life.

"For whatever is born of God overcomes the world; and this is the victory that has overcome the world—our faith. And who is the one who overcomes the world, but he who believes that Jesus is the Son of God?" (1 John 5:4–5).

Greater Works. Jesus said that because He was going to the Father—and because He was giving us the Holy Spirit—we would do the works He did, and even greater. (See John 14:12.)

God's Children. "For all who are being led by the Spirit of God, these are sons of God," Paul wrote in Romans 8:14.

Earlier in John's Gospel we read: "But as many as received Him, to them He gave the right to become children of God, even to those who believe in His name, who were born not of blood, nor of the will of the flesh, nor of the will of man, but of God" (John 1:12–13).

When Jesus baptizes the believer with His

Holy Spirit, He brings all these benefits and more into his life. Can we do any less than to receive with obedience, joy, and thanksgiving all that God desires to give us?

Chapter 7

HANDLING "RIGHTS"

As new creatures, we learn to live for Christ and no longer for ourselves. In addition, God desires that we allow Him to bring into our lives those circumstances that may not be pleasant, recognizing that God loves us and wants us to grow to maturity.

The apostle Paul wrote in 2 Corinthians 5: 14–15: "The love of Christ controls us, having concluded this, that one died for all, therefore all died; and He died for all, that they who live should no longer live for themselves, but for Him who died and rose again on their behalf."

Learning how to handle our rights is one facet of growing toward spiritual maturity.

7.1 OUR "RIGHTS"

What do we consider our rights to be? We can say that we have the right to be respected by our employer. Or that we have the right to our reputation, whether good or bad. We may also say regarding those personal belongings God has given us, "They're mine. It's my right to keep them and not share them." And so we hang on to what we consider *ours* .

We also believe we have a right to our security. God may ask us to give up the security we place in a home, job or any earthly, material thing.

God wants to provide for all our needs, but He does not want us to focus our affections on those things He gives us. Only God, and not our jobs or our paychecks, is our source. The things He gives us are simply part of His provision to meet our needs.

7.2 DO WE, AS CHRISTIANS, HAVE RIGHTS?

Mark 10:17–22 records the story of a rich man who came to Jesus and asked Him what he must do to inherit eternal life. Jesus reminded him of the commandments, which the man said he had kept from his youth.

"And looking at him, Jesus felt a love for him, and said to him, 'One thing you lack: go and sell all you possess, and give it to the poor, and you shall have treasure in heaven; and come, follow Me.' But at these words his face fell, and he went away grieved, for he was one who owned much property" (verses 21–22).

The man simply did not want to give up all he had. He did not believe Jesus had the right to take it all away. So he went away sorrowful.

When we deny Christ the right to our lives, we also go away sorrowful, and our countenance reveals it. When we hang on to our rights, to self, which denies and displeases Him, our spirit is bound to reflect it in our countenance.

We must be willing simply to give up our rights, our all, to Jesus.

7.3 HOW DO WE YIELD OUR RIGHTS?

Yielding our rights is not an easy step, but one that is necessary to our growth. In John's Gospel

Jesus states: "Truly, truly, I say to you, unless a grain of wheat falls into the earth and dies, it remains by itself alone; but if it dies, it bears much fruit. He who loves his life loses it; and he who hates his life in this world shall keep it to life eternal" (John 12:24–25).

The hardest thing for us to do is to die to self. Can we ever think we have completely accomplished this? In the process of being sanctified, God is polishing and perfecting us. Therefore, we must die daily. God will allow us to go through difficult circumstances to bring us to that goal of spiritual maturity and to get our undivided attention.

We must, first of all, identify the right that needs to be yielded; that thing, such as our security; or even perhaps a person to whom we are clinging. We need to confess that specifically to God.

We must transfer that right to God, asking Him to forgive us for hanging onto earthly security or a spouse or whatever it might be, and repent of it. We will then be free to say, "Lord, I give that right to You."

Finally we can thank Him, whatever the outcome. If we give up that right to Him, without murmuring and complaining, God has promised He will bless us.

7.4 WHAT HAPPENS WHEN WE YIELD OUR RIGHTS?

In Philippians 2:5–11, we see the perfect example of yielded rights. Jesus emptied Himself of His power and took the form of a servant. He humbled Himself and became obedient to the point of death. And He died. Jesus demonstrated the process of dying to self.

Because of Jesus' obedience, God highly exalted Him. He bestowed on Jesus a name above every name and brought to Him great honor.

God blesses us when we obey Him. Jesus could have said, "Father, You do not have the right to ask Me to go to Calvary." But, being perfect, He responded out of obedience, and God blessed Him.

Oswald Chambers, author of *My Utmost for His Highest*, once said that "the stamp of the saint is that he can waive his own rights and obey the Lord Jesus."

Giving our rights to God, patiently, daily, is another step in the life that is moving toward spiritual maturity.

Chapter 8

FINDING GOD'S WILL

Every day each of us is faced with making decisions. We want to do what is best, but sometimes it is difficult to know just what *is* best.

Man's way is to determine with his mind what he should do, whereas God's way is to direct a man's heart. Proverbs 16:9 says, "The mind of man plans his way, but the Lord directs his steps." We also read in Proverbs 21:1: "The king's heart is like channels of water in the hand of the Lord; He turns it wherever He wishes."

And we have that promise in Proverbs 3:6 that if we acknowledge the Lord in all our ways, He will direct our paths.

If we follow man's way and determine with our mind what to do, then we will miss God's will. But if we let Him direct our hearts, then we will know His will for our lives.

8.1 SIMPLE STEPS IN FINDING GUIDANCE

We must first ask God for wisdom. He has promised to give us the wisdom we need. (See James 1:5.)

The apostle John states, "And we receive from Him whatever we ask for, because we (watchfully) obey His orders—observe His suggestions and injunctions, follow His plan for us—and (habitually) practice what is pleasing to Him" (1 John 3:22, The Amplified Bible).

Just as we must listen to another person who gives us directions, so we must listen to God when He directs us. We can train our hearts to hear His quiet voice speaking, whether through His written word, through circumstances, through godly counsel, or through a gentle leading in our hearts.

Isaiah prophesied, "And your ears will hear a word behind you, 'This is the way, walk in it,' whenever you turn to the right or to the left" (Isaiah 30:21).

If we need help in making a particular decision, it is good to seek godly counsel. Even simply opening our heart to someone wiser than we can turn us in the right direction. Solomon declared, "Where there is no guidance, the people fall, But in abundance of counselors there is victory" (Proverbs 11:14).

We do not have to be anxious about God showing us His will, for He is the one who works in us "to will and to work for His good pleasure" (Philippians 2:13).

8.2 RENEWING THE MIND

For God to direct us, we need to establish a program for renewing our mind so that we are not conformed to the habits and thought patterns of this world. God's Word is very explicit concerning where our battle is won or lost, that is, in the mind.

Ephesians 6:12 says, "Our struggle is not against flesh and blood, but against the spiritual forces of wickedness." Where do we begin? A good place is with the Word which tells us to take "every thought captive to the obedience of Christ" (2 Corinthians 10:5).

How can we do this? Let's look to the Word again. "Whatever is true, whatever is honorable, whatever is right, whatever is pure, whatever is lovely, whatever is of good repute, if there is any excellence and if anything worthy of praise, let your mind dwell on these things" (Philippians 4:8).

Psalm 119:11 also says, "Thy word I have treasured in my heart, That I may not sin against Thee."

8.3 ACCEPTING HIS BEST

Because we know beyond a shadow of a doubt that God's will is best for us, we seek His will above ours.

In the Garden of Gethsemane before His crucifixion, Jesus expressed His true feelings to His Father: "Father, if Thou art willing, remove this cup from Me." But He added immediately, "Yet not My will, but Thine be done." (Luke 22:42). Jesus was honest, but He also submitted His will to the Father's.

In Jeremiah 29:11–13, we find this promise from the God who directs our hearts and our steps: " 'For I know the plans that I have for you,' declares the Lord, 'plans for welfare and not for calamity to give you a future and a hope. . . . And you will seek Me and find Me, when you search for Me with all your heart.' "

Let us remember, then, the psalmist's words: "I delight to do Thy will, O my God; Thy Law is within my heart" (Psalm 40:8).

Chapter 9

PRAYER AND FASTING

Prayer and fasting are two important elements of the Christian's life that will enable him to grow toward spiritual maturity. Failure to develop a disciplined prayer life or to exercise the principles of fasting will result in a dry, ineffective Christian walk.

9.1 DISCIPLINED PRAYER LIFE

Jesus went to Gethsemane to pray, taking His disciples with Him. He left them alone, telling them to keep watch and pray. But when He returned, they were sleeping. "Couldn't you watch with Me for one hour?" He asked them. (See Matthew 26:36–40.)

With this challenge in mind, I would like to offer the following twelve-step plan as a guide to help you fill one hour with five-minute segments of meaningful prayer. (The resource material was obtained from Change the World Ministries.)

Everyone prays differently, and some will omit one or more of these segments. Some segments may be shorter, others longer. Remember, this is only a suggested guide.

But set a pattern with which you and the Lord are comfortable. And at all costs, discipline yourself to pray.

Praise. All prayer should begin with a recognition of God's nature. The Lord's Prayer—our model for all praying—begins with the words "Our Father who art in heaven, hallowed be Thy name" (Matthew 6:9).

In praise we esteem God for His nature and accomplishments. (See Psalm 63:3 and Hebrews 13:15.)

Waiting. Not only should we begin prayer with praise, but we should give time to being quiet in God's presence.

The original Hebrew text of Psalm 37:7—"Rest in the Lord,"—means "Be still" in the Lord. This is not meditation, or just a time for listening. It is simply taking time to let God love you.

(See also Isaiah 40:31 and Lamentations 3:25.)

Confession. The psalmist asked God to search his heart for unconfessed sin. He knew that sin was one of the greatest roadblocks to answered prayer.

Early in prayer we need to make time for confession. This clears the way for powerful praying to a God who answers. (See Psalm 51:10–11; Psalm 66:18; Psalm 139:23–24; 1 John 1:9.)

Reading the Word. "The commandment of the Lord [God's Word] is pure, enlightening the eyes," wrote King David (Psalm 19:8). When we bring God's Word into our prayer, we open our eyes to new possibilities in God.

At this point in our prayer, we might want to read God's Word. (See 2 Timothy 3:16.)

Intercession. Our praying now centers on interceding for a lost and dying world and for others who have desperate needs.

Intercession is one aspect of prayer in which five minutes will never be enough. It involves a travail of the soul that will lead us into the very heart of God. As we intercede for others, God will lay as a burden on our hearts what is also on His heart, and we ourselves will be changed. (See 1 Timothy 2:1–2; Psalm 2:8; Matthew 9:37–38.)

Petition. This aspect of prayer concerns our personal needs. The Lord's Prayer includes petition in the expression "Give us this day our daily bread."

To petition God is to open our hearts to Him through prayer and present our needs. (See Matthew 6:11; Matthew 7:7; James 4:2.)

Praying the Word. Bringing God's Word into prayer is so important that it appears twice on the list. I suggested reading God's Word as the step after confession. Now I am recommending *praying* God's Word, bringing actual Scripture verses into our prayer. We cannot pray out of God's will when we pray His Word. (See 2 Samuel 22:31; Numbers 23:19.)

Thanksgiving. When Paul wrote to the Philippians, he instructed them to offer "prayer and supplication *with thanksgiving*" (Philippians 4:6, italics added). Thus, thanksgiving should occupy more than a single aspect of prayer; it should be sprinkled throughout.

Thanksgiving differs from praise in that praise recognizes God for who He is, while thanksgiving recognizes God for specific things He has done. (See Psalm 100:4.)

Singing. Melody in its truest sense is a gift of God for the purpose of singing praises unto Him.

Many Christians, sadly, have never learned the beauty of singing a "new song" to God during prayer. These songs may come straight from the heart, with the Holy Spirit creating the melody.

Paul wrote of "spiritual songs" (Ephesians 5:19). To sing to the Lord in spiritual songs is to worship God in melody. (See Psalm 100:2 and Psalm 144:9.)

Meditation. To wait in God's presence, as noted earlier, is simply to be there to love Him. Meditation differs from waiting in that our minds during meditation are very active.

To meditate is to ponder spiritual themes that refer to God. Only once in Scripture do we find God specifically promising success and prosperity: As gifts to those who meditate day and night in His Word (Joshua 1:8; see also Psalm 1:1–3; Psalm 77:12.)

Listening. Whether through His written Word or by the inner still, small voice of the Holy Spirit, God speaks to praying Christians. But we must take time to listen.

Listening is different from both waiting and meditation. Here we listen for direct orders from our heavenly Father concerning our daily activities. (See 1 Kings 19:11–13; Ecclesiastes 5:2.)

Praise. An imaginary door to every prayer time carries a sign that reads *Praise*. We must always enter prayer through this door. And when prayer draws to its conclusion, we must look for the same door.

As we begin prayer by recognizing God's nature, we end in a similar fashion. Jesus taught this when He ended His prayer with the statement

"For Thine is the kingdom, and the power, and the glory, forever. Amen" (Matthew 6:13; see also Psalm 100:4 and Psalm 150.)

This simple, twelve-step plan for filling an hour with meaningful prayer is just a suggestion. Everyone has a different prayer life. But each one of us must discipline ourselves to prayer in order to reach our fullest potential in Jesus Christ.

9.2 GUIDELINES FOR FASTING

Fasting as a spiritual exercise teaches us to depend on God for our strength rather than on food. The following principles will help us as we fast.

It is better to begin fasting when we are spiritually "up" than to wait for an emergency. God moves us from strength to strength (Psalm 84:7); from faith to faith (Romans 1:17); and from glory to glory (2 Corinthians 3:18).

We should enter into fasting with a lively faith, remembering that "without faith it is impossible to please Him, for he who comes to God must believe that He is, and that He is a rewarder of those who seek Him" (Hebrews 11:6; see also Romans 10:17).

We should not begin with too long a period of fasting. Omitting a few meals, and then moving on gradually to longer periods as God directs, will prevent discouragement.

During the fast, we need to devote ourselves to periods of Bible reading and prayer to allow the Holy Spirit to strengthen us and give us special insights. Setting certain objectives in fasting by making a list will build our faith as God honors the fast and we see those objectives met.

Too, we must avoid boastfulness during the time of fasting. Our lives should remain outwardly normal and routine, as Jesus urged:

"And whenever you fast, do not put on a gloomy face as the hypocrites do, for they neglect their appearance in order to be seen fasting by men. Truly I say to you, they have their reward in full. But you, when you fast, anoint your head, and wash your face so that you may not be seen fasting by men, but by your Father who is in secret; and your Father who sees in secret will repay you" (Matthew 6:16–18).

Finally, we need to check our motives carefully. Each time of fasting must be inspired by the Holy Spirit and follow God's Word.

9.3 PHYSICAL BENEFITS OF FASTING

In addition to its spiritual dimension, fasting has certain physical aspects. Since our bodies are the temple of the Holy Spirit, fasting will cleanse and remove toxic materials from our systems. (If a person is on medication, it is important to consult a physician before attempting to fast, even for a limited period.)

Early in a fast, unpleasant physical symptoms such as dizziness, headaches, or nausea, may occur. This discomfort should not discourage us. Our systems are being purged of impurities. In the case of a longer fast, these physical reactions should pass after the first two or three days. Hunger, which in part is a habit, will also pass if we continue in the fast.

During a fast, some people drink only water. Others take various kinds of fluid, such as fruit juice, broth or skim milk. We need to work out the pattern of fasting that suits us best, as the Lord grants us wisdom.

If a person abstains from all fluids, he should limit his fast to 72 hours. To exceed this limit can cause disastrous physical effects.

We should break a fast gradually, beginning with light meals that are easy to digest. Self-control is important here. Eating too heavily can cause physical discomfort and can nullify the physical benefits of fasting.

If a fast exceeds two days, a person's stomach will shrink and should not be over-expanded. If we train ourselves to eat lighter meals, our stomachs will adjust accordingly.

Chapter 10

TRIALS AND SUFFERING

As we mentioned earlier, God allows unpleasant circumstances in our lives to bring us to spiritual maturity. These circumstances may come in the form of trials and suffering, which we all experience.

10.1 TYPES OF TRIALS

Let us examine some different types of trials.

General. Paul describes general types of trials in this way: "Who shall separate us from the love of Christ? Shall tribulation, or distress, or persecution, or famine, or nakedness, or peril, or sword? Just as it is written, 'For Thy sake we are being put to death all day long; we were considered as sheep to be slaughtered'" (Romans 8:35–36).

Persecution. Jesus said in the Sermon on the Mount, "Blessed are you when men revile you, and persecute you, and say all kinds of evil against you falsely, on account of Me. Rejoice, and be glad, for your reward in heaven is great, for so they persecuted the prophets who were before you" (Matthew 5:11–12).

Most of us have not experienced or do not know what real persecution is like. But Jesus, who was nailed to the cross, who gave up all for us, surely knows what it means to suffer real persecution.

Persecution can take many forms. We can be spit upon, cursed, shot, or experience some other form of insult that we would understand to be persecution. We do, however, have the promise from Jesus of a reward in heaven.

Afflictions. We can also be afflicted by many things that God allows to keep us from exalting ourselves. Paul experienced this firsthand:

"And because of the surpassing greatness of the revelations, for this reason, to keep me from exalting myself, there was given me a thorn in the flesh, a messenger of Satan to buffet me—to keep me from exalting myself!" (2 Corinthians 12:7).

God wants to keep us humble, contrite and broken, so that we will listen to His voice and depend on Him. When we are in a position of brokenness and humility before the Lord, we are singleminded. Unfortunately, we move back and forth between humility and pride. Afflictions achieve the godly purpose of driving us to our knees before Him.

Chastisement. When God chastises or disciplines us, He does it for our good. As the writer of Hebrews said, "My son, do not regard lightly the discipline of the Lord, Nor faint when you are reproved by Him; For those whom the Lord loves He disciplines, And He scourges every son whom He receives" (Hebrews 12:5–6).

Whether it be a general trial, persecution, affliction, or chastisement, it comes our way because the Lord sees a way of expressing His love to us. Otherwise He would let us go our own way without correction or redirection. Trials come, then, because God loves us.

10.2 SOURCES OF TRIALS

People. People—individuals or groups—can be our biggest source of trials.

Circumstances. Trials may also arise in the circumstances that surround us—whether on our jobs, in our communities or cities, or even in our homes.

Self. Sometimes we are our own worst enemy. We battle ourselves when God wants us to love ourselves. He created us, and our bodies are the temple of the Holy Spirit.

10.3 RESULTS OF TRIALS

What character trait does God want to develop in us through trials? The apostle Peter gives us an idea:

"For what credit is there if, when you sin and are harshly treated, you endure it with patience? But if when you do what is right and suffer for it you patiently endure it, this finds favor with God. For you have been called for this purpose, since Christ also suffered for you, leaving you an example for you to follow in His steps" (1 Peter 2:20–21).

Many Christians believe we do not have to suffer, but that is contrary to what God teaches us in His Word. Suffering is part of Scripture. And, according to God's Word, it is part of our human existence. Jesus suffered and died for us. We too will suffer.

10.4 PAUL'S EXAMPLE

God wants us to overcome in every trial or difficult circumstance. Paul showed us how he responded to trials:

"We are afflicted in every way, but not crushed; perplexed, but not despairing; persecuted, but not forsaken; struck down, but not destroyed; always carrying about in the body the dying of Jesus, that the life of Jesus also may be manifested in our body. For we who live are constantly being delivered over to death for Jesus' sake, that the life of Jesus also may be manifested in our mortal flesh. So death works in us, but life in you" (2 Corinthians 4:8-12).

God wants us to respond in the same way. Paul said that he was not crushed; perplexed but not driven to despair; persecuted but not forsaken. We can depend on God, who has told us that He will never leave us or forsake us (see Hebrews 13:5), and that nothing can separate us from His love (Romans 8:38-39).

We may ask God to take us out of the difficult circumstances. But He alone knows when we are ready, and when He has accomplished His purposes in those trials.

10.5 TRIALS OF LIFE

God desires that we respond in a godly way to the day-to-day trials we encounter. When we meet unlovable people, God wants us to love them. He may direct us to go to someone and ask forgiveness. Our unloving attitude can hinder God's working in that person's life, while love can help to bring him or her to a saving knowledge of Christ.

Another reason God allows us to go through these experiences is to build in us the strength of the Holy Spirit. In His power we learn to live as overcomers so that we can experience and show forth His joy in the midst of sorrow; His peace in the midst of confusion; His generosity in time of need; His flexibility when we are inconvenienced; His forgiveness even when we are used despitefully; His strength when we are tempted. Because God is the Creator of the universe, nothing touches our lives that has not passed His hand.

Job in the Old Testament illustrates this fact. Satan had no freedom in Job's life until God lifted the hedge and gave him permission.

When it seems that our own rights are intruded upon, we must surrender those rights.

When we face unwelcome responsibilities, God wants to develop trustworthiness in us, so that we can be trusted with anything He brings our way. If we cannot be trusted, He keeps working with us. So it is with trials. If we do not learn a lesson the first time, God will allow more and more trials in our lives until we do.

10.6 PURPOSE OF TRIALS

James explains God's purpose in trials: "Consider it all joy, my brethren, when you encounter various trials, knowing that the testing of your faith produces endurance. And let endurance have its perfect result, that you may be perfect and complete, lacking in nothing" (James 1:2–4).

God desires that we be complete, mature Christians. He uses the trials to mold us into His image. (See Hebrews 12:3–11.)

10.7 RESPONSE TO TRIALS

God is more concerned about our response to trials than He is about the actual trials. Will we grumble and murmur? Or will we consider them "all joy"?

When we look to God, setting our minds "on the things above, not on the things that are on earth" (Colossians 3:2), we will overcome in the trials. When we focus on the trial itself, we become discouraged and defeated.

God has promised in Psalm 34:19, "Many are the afflictions of the righteous; but the Lord delivers him out of them all."

We need to believe that. God never forsakes us, and He desires that we overcome in our trials. "But in all these things," Paul tells us, "we overwhelmingly conquer through Him who loved us" (Romans 8:37).

And the apostle John encourages us: "For this is the love of God, that we keep His commandments; and His commandments are not burdensome. For whatever is born of God overcomes the world; and this is the victory that has overcome the world—our faith" (1 John 5:3–4).

When counseling someone, we will want to help them to identify the trial, identify the source, respond correctly, and thank God for both His victory and His presence. (See 2 Corinthians 6:3–10; 11:23–29; 1 Peter 4:12–19; James 5:10–11; John 16:33; 2 Corinthians 12:10; Romans 5:3–5.)

10.8 PRINCIPLES OF SUFFERING

Out of trials comes suffering. Paul wrote to the Philippian church: "For to you it has been granted for Christ's sake, not only to believe in Him, but also to suffer for His sake" (Philippians 1:29).

Jesus learned obedience through suffering. We too learn obedience in following His example.

As a believer sometimes falters in his walk with God, God in His love sometimes finds it necessary to discipline and chastise that believer in order to produce "the peaceful fruit of righteousness" in his life. (See Hebrews 12:11.)

10.9 AREAS OF SUFFERING

We may suffer in an area such as finances, which might result in a loss of earning power, loss of job, or even poverty.

Some of the most severe suffering may come within our families. One's spouse, children, parents, or relatives may encounter illness, death, divorce, loss of faith, rebellion against God, financial difficulties, or other family-related problems.

10.10 NATURAL RESPONSES TO SUFFERING

A person may respond naturally to suffering with a troubled spirit. His mind may be filled with worry and doubt, his will fraught with constant indecision, his emotions unbalanced. A physiological reaction may manifest in illness or physical impairment.

10.11 GOD'S FOURFOLD PURPOSE FOR SUFFERING

"After you have suffered for a little," Peter wrote, "the God of all grace, who called you to

His eternal glory in Christ, will Himself perfect, confirm, strengthen and establish you" (1 Peter 5:10).

Perfection speaks of completion, of being complete in Christ, just as suffering confirms or verifies our relationship with Him.

And suffering establishes us. It sets us on the solid Rock, Jesus, and makes us firm in our faith, with the end result that God is glorified. We don't ask, "Why me?" We already know why.

10.12 BIBLICAL RESPONSE TO SUFFERING

We are to rejoice in our suffering. As Peter wrote:

"Beloved, do not be surprised at the fiery ordeal among you, which comes upon you for your testing, as though some strange thing were happening to you; but to the degree that you share the sufferings of Christ, keep on rejoicing; so that also at the revelation of His glory, you may rejoice with exultation. If you are reviled for the name of Christ, you are blessed, because the Spirit of glory and of God rests upon you" (1 Peter 4:12–14).

(See also Philippians 3:10–11 and Romans 8:16–18.)

10.13 GROWTH THROUGH TRIALS AND SUFFERING

Trials and suffering can be our greatest motivation for spiritual growth—*or* our deadliest means of discouragement. The difference depends upon our understanding of God's purposes through the trials.

Trials and suffering can bring about the following invaluable spiritual results:

Reveal our weaknesses (see 1 Corinthians 1:26–29).

Reveal God's love for us (see Hebrews 12:6).

Cause us to examine our hearts (see Psalm 139:23–24).

Help us overcome pride (see James 4:6).

Change our focus (see Psalm 25:1–2).

Cause us to seek God (see Psalm 86:3).

Help us recognize spiritual warfare (see Ephesians 6:12).

Purify our faith (see James 1:3–4).

Cause us to hate evil (see Proverbs 8:13).

Remind us to pray for our authorities (see 1 Thessalonians 5:12–13).

Cause us to reevaluate our priorities (see 2 Corinthians 4:18).

Test our work (see 1 Corinthians 3:12–15).

Sift and evaluate our friendships (see Proverbs 17:17).

Help us identify with Christ (see Galatians 2:20).

Reveal our accountability (see Proverbs 16:6).

Motivate us to comfort others (see 2 Corinthians 1:3–5).

Let us comfort and encourage one another, with the knowledge that God is in control in both trials and sufferings, to the end that we may grow in maturity of spirit.

Chapter 11

DEVELOPING GODLY ATTITUDES AND CHARACTER

Our attitudes arise out of day-to-day experiences and either please or displease God, depending on our response. Circumstances do not produce attitudes; rather, attitudes result from our responses to those circumstances, whether they be conflicts, trials, or sufferings.

According to Jesus, "There is nothing outside the man which going into him can defile him; but the things which proceed out of the man are what defile the man" (Mark 7:15).

God has a plan for each one of us. The circumstances we encounter, therefore, are designed to perfect us. It is often easier for us to encourage other people with the following verse than it is to believe it for ourselves: "And we know that God causes all things to work together for good to those who love God, to those who are called according to His purpose" (Romans 8:28; see also Matthew 5:11–12).

God wants to produce in us the character of Christ, so that we will set our minds (as we have already seen) "on the things above, not on the things that are on earth" (Colossians 3:2). And it is that character in us, that attitude or response to circumstances, that others will see. Our attitudes can determine how effective or ineffective our witness will be.

Jesus declared in the Sermon on the Mount, "Let your light shine before men in such a way that they may see your good works, and glorify your Father who is in heaven" (Matthew 5:16).

Out of each circumstance, we make a decision of the will (soul); and that decision is either ungodly or godly.

11.1 UNGODLY ATTITUDE

If we grumble or complain when going through an unpleasant or difficult circumstance, we develop an ungodly attitude. That ungodly attitude produces an ungodly action and an ungodly witness. Other people do not enjoy being around us because of our attitude, action, and witness. Worse, we can move far away from God.

The Old Testament gives us an example of an ungodly attitude that ended in tragedy: "And the whole congregation of the sons of Israel grumbled against Moses and Aaron in the wilderness" (Exodus 16:2). This ungodly attitude, as they continued to grumble and complain about their circumstances, kept the children of Israel wandering for forty years in the wilderness, where they eventually died.

11.2 GODLY ATTITUDE

God desires that in all circumstances we have a godly attitude, which produces a godly action and, in turn, a godly witness.

Forgiveness is a godly attitude. Jesus gave us the best example of a godly attitude. When He was hanging on the cross, life draining out of Him, He prayed, "Father forgive them; for they do not know what they are doing" (Luke 23:34).

That is the kind of attitude God wants us to have. It produces a godly witness.

Although we fail many times in our response to circumstances we must always remember God's promise in 2 Corinthians 12:9: "My grace is sufficient for you, for power is perfected in weakness."

God's grace is sufficient when we fail. But we do not want to test Him just to see how much grace He will extend to us. God desires that we walk according to His way today and not wait until tomorrow.

Whenever we recognize an ungodly attitude in ourselves, whenever we fail in our actions, we need to confess it as sin. For God is faithful "to forgive us our sins and to cleanse us from all unrighteousness" (1 John 1:9). He cleans the slate, never to bring our failures up to us again.

11.3 GODLY HABITS AND CHARACTER

How do we develop godly habits and character? How do we let godly attitude responses become patterns?

As Paul wrote, "Do you not know that when you present yourselves to someone as slaves for obedience, you are slaves of the one whom you obey, either of sin resulting in death, or of obedience resulting in righteousness?" (Romans 6:16).

We must first lay aside the ungodly attitude or habit and learn a new way of responding and acting. We can renew our minds by studying and meditating on Scripture verses that pertain to our problems and show us God's way. And we must begin to respond and act according to those biblical attitudes and behavior patterns.

Since most changes take time, we must also discipline ourselves by being faithful each day to practice the new attitudes and habits. Godly character will result and we will be an example to others, for as God's Word promises, "in speech, conduct, love, faith and purity, show yourself an example of those who believe" (1 Timothy 4:12).

(See Ephesians 4:20–24; 1 Timothy 4:7; 2 Peter 1:1–11; 1 Thessalonians 5:23; Galatians 5:22–23.)

Chapter 12

HEALING

Healing is probably one of the least understood areas of the Christian faith. The question often arises, "Why are some healed and others not?" Most Christians would respond, "I don't know."

Others sometimes respond, "The reason a person is not healed is that he doesn't have enough faith."

Whether or not a person experiences physical healing, we must first recognize that God has many purposes—some of them mysterious to us— as we press on toward spiritual maturity.

What is God's will in any given situation in which we think healing is needed? Can we "make" God perform according to His Word? Is all sickness of Satan or because of sin? What about sickness caused by our own foolishness or by organic causes? Is lack of faith the only thing standing between God and supernatural healing? Does consulting a physician or taking medicine show a lack of faith? Should we say we are healed even when symptoms are still present?

These are some of the questions one may ask about healing. Even though we do not have definitive answers to all of these questions, we know God does. As Jesus said, "With men it is impossible, but not with God; for all things are possible with God" (Mark 10:27).

Jesus healed all those who came to Him. And we can trust Him to heal us today, because "Jesus Christ is the same yesterday and today, yes and forever" (Hebrews 13:8).

Jesus never changes, and God's Word promises healing, so we must keep His Word in our hearts, since it is "life to those who find [it], and health to all their whole body." (See Proverbs 4:20–22.) God heals us spiritually, emotionally, and physically.

12.1 PRINCIPLES OF HEALING

Let's look at some principles of healing.

First, our healing comes through a life that is surrendered to Jesus Christ. God can and does heal the non-Christian for His own purposes. But for the most part, healing comes through a life of obedience, a personal commitment to Jesus Christ, and a willingness to resolve sin.

In Exodus we read: "If you will give earnest heed to the voice of the Lord your God, and do what is right in His sight, and give ear to His commandments, and keep all His statutes, I will put none of the diseases on you which I have put on the Egyptians; for I, the Lord, am your healer" (Exodus 15:26).

The Bible also states, on the other hand, that sickness is a curse resulting from disobedience: "But it shall come about, if you will not obey the Lord your God, to observe to do all His commandments and His statutes which I charge you today, that all these curses shall come upon you and overtake you" (Deuteronomy 28:15).

We can, however, move from the old to the new covenant, in which we find that "Christ redeemed us from the curse of the Law, having become a curse for us—for it is written, 'Cursed is every one who hangs on a tree'" (Galatians 3:13; see also 3 John 2.)

Furthermore, this redemption was provided as part of the atoning work of Christ (see Isaiah 53:4–5). And this awesome work included salvation from sickness and infirmity.

During Jesus' earthly ministry, He sent out His disciples to multiply His work, making them instruments of healing. They were given authority "to heal every kind of disease and every kind of sickness" (Matthew 10:1). They did not possess any special privileges, but with God's Spirit working in and through them, they could bring healing to those in need. (See Matthew 10:8; Mark 16:17–18; Luke 9:2, 10:8–9.)

Healing is one of the nine major "ministry" gifts of the Spirit, as recorded in 1 Corinthians 12:9: "To another faith by the same Spirit, and to another gifts of healing by the one Spirit." (See also 1 Corinthians 12:28.)

"All do not have gifts of healing, do they?" asks the apostle Paul (See 1 Corinthians 12:30). All believers do *not* have the gifts of healing, as their personal gift, however, during their lifetimes all the gifts can flow through their lives as God sees the need and releases His power. As believers we *can* pray the prayer of faith for that one who is afflicted, knowing that God hears and that His power is able to heal those who are sick.

12.2 METHODS OF HEALING

The healings recorded in Scripture came through many different methods. Jesus Himself used more than one means to heal the sick. No matter what the method, however, we must always remember it is God who heals.

Prayer of Faith. God heals through the prayer of faith. The writer of Hebrews tells us that "faith is the assurance of things hoped for, the conviction of things not seen" (Hebrews 11:1).

We know that faith, in turn, "comes from hearing, and hearing by the word of Christ" (Romans 10:17).

According to James 5:15, "The prayer offered in faith will restore the one who is sick, and the Lord will raise him up, and if he has committed sins, they will be forgiven him."

We must acknowledge it is God's will to heal us. The question is how and when. It requires faith and not presumption. We dare not put God to a foolish test.

The key to healing is knowing that, as the James passage makes clear, *the Lord* will raise him up. It is not within our power to raise a sick person up, but it is within God's power.

Medical Intervention. Let us say at once that God may choose to heal through physicians and prescriptions. Some say going to a doctor or using a prescription shows a lack of faith. Yet Jesus recognized the time and place for doctors: "It is not those who are well who need a physician, but those who are sick" (Luke 5:31). Luke, the great Gospelist and author of the power-filled book of Acts, was himself a physician. (See Colossians 4:14.)

Many Christian doctors will pray and seek the Lord first with the patient, and then do whatever He directs. Seeking His direction is all-important.

For God may choose to heal in a number of ways. Whatever path he chooses we must follow his guidance in order to receive our healing.

Instantaneous. God also heals directly through His Word, both instantly and progressively. In Matthew 8:5–13 we read an account of instantaneous healing, in the story of the centurion whose servant lay paralyzed and in great pain at home. When Jesus said He would go and heal him, the centurion replied, "Lord, I am not qualified for You to come under my roof, but just say the word, and my servant will be healed" (verse 8).

"Go your way," Jesus responded; "let it be done to you as you have believed." And the servant was healed "that very hour" (verse 13). (See also Matthew 12:10–13; Psalm 107:20.)

Progressive. In another case Jesus healed a person progressively. Mark's Gospel gives the account of a blind man who was brought to Jesus.

"And taking the blind man by the hand, He brought him out of the village; and after spitting on his eyes, and laying His hands upon him, He asked him, 'Do you see anything?' And he looked up and said, "I see men, for I am seeing them like trees, walking about." Then again He laid His hands upon his eyes; and he looked intently and was restored, and began to see everything clearly" (Mark 8:23–25).

At the point when he could see men like trees, he did not yet have a complete healing. It did not mean Jesus was any less powerful or that His first touch was not enough. Rather, it was done this way for His purpose.

Others' Faith. God heals in answer to the faith of others.

Mark 2:1–5 also records the story of the paralytic who was let down on a pallet through the roof by four men: "And Jesus seeing their faith said to the paralytic, 'My son, your sins are forgiven'" (verse 5; see also Matthew 9:2–7).

Despite Unbelief. God heals at times in spite of our unbelief. God is God. He sees the overall "big picture" and can heal in any way He chooses. Jesus performed many signs and miracles before the people of His day, yet they did not believe in Him (see John 12:37). We know that many people, on the other hand, both then and now, have come to believe in Him as a result of being healed.

When Elders Pray. God heals in answer to the prayers of the elders of the church.

James offers this familiar instruction: "Is anyone among you sick? Let him call for the elders of the church, and let them pray over him, anointing him with oil in the name of the Lord" (James 5:14).

God wants us to obey His Word. He wants to prove His Word to us. He desires that we be humble before Him and open to His method of healing, not locked in to only one method. He heals in many different ways, and His Word works. (See Mark 16:17–18.)

12.3 HINDRANCES TO HEALING

We know God heals through the prayer of faith, physicians, medicine, His Word or any method He chooses. But we also see that not everyone is healed. Let's look at some possible hindrances to healing.

Sin. Sin is a major hindrance to healing. Bitterness, resentment, unforgiveness, or even occult activities all block God's healing. James exhorts us to "confess your sins to one another . . . so that you may be healed. The effective prayer of a righteous man can accomplish much" (James 5:16).

In 1 Corinthians 11:28–30 Paul wrote that many of the believers at Corinth were "weak and sick, and a number sleep" because they did not "judge the body rightly" when they came to partake of holy Communion.

A university medical doctor reported that many of those "sitting in doctors' waiting rooms have nothing organically wrong with them. Their illness is psychosomatic. Their negative thinking, their unresolved hostilities and anxieties, broke through the immunity factor and illness overtook them."

Thus, unresolved sin can cause psychosomatic illness that hinders our being healed. (See Psalm 32:1–4; Psalm 38:3; Matthew 9:2–7.)

God's Glory. God allows afflictions to continue for a time to fulfill His own purposes.

Jesus said of the man born blind, "It was neither that this man sinned, nor his parents; but it was in order that the works of God might be displayed in him" (John 9:3).

The man was blind not because of sin, but because God wanted to reveal Himself through the man's affliction. Some people may not think that is love, but we do not know how many people will be touched in a positive way through another's illness.

When Jesus heard that his friend Lazarus was

sick, He responded, "This sickness is not unto death, but for the glory of God, that the Son of God may be glorified by it" (John 11:4). Jesus knew God would receive the glory when He raised Lazarus from the dead, and He was willing to wait for that time.

God is sovereign. He makes no mistakes and His timing is perfect. He wants to glorify Himself in all things. And He has promised that nothing can separate us from His love. (Romans 8:35–39.) When we see someone suffering from a life-threatening illness, we may not see that as love, but we need to trust the wisdom and sovereignty of God and know that He will produce fruit from that illness that brings glory to His name.

God's Power in Us. God can perfect His power in our weakness.

We have already discussed the apostle Paul's "thorn in the flesh," which God used for His purposes (see 2 Corinthians 12:7–10). Part of God's purpose was to keep Paul from exalting himself. Another purpose was that God could perfect His power in Paul's weakness.

Considerable speculation has been offered as to what Paul's thorn in the flesh was. Some believe it was a physical affliction, while others believe it was a demonic spirit sent to buffet him.

Whatever it was, God allowed it to continue after Paul petitioned Him three times to remove it from him. Paul acknowledged that God had revealed to him that His grace was sufficient, and that when he was weak, in Christ he became strong.

Sometimes God has to allow a circumstance in our lives, too, to keep us humble. If we don't want to be humble, God will find a way to humble us anyway. He loves us that much and wants our undivided attention.

God's Perfect Healing. Healing may be delayed or even lead to "perfect healing" if God desires to take a person home. His purpose might be to touch others' lives through that person's faith and life, thereby causing others to accept Christ as their Lord and Savior or to be freed from the power of sin.

We should always release individuals or circumstances to God's care while believing and trusting God to heal in His own way and in His timing. We do not want to limit God nor tell Him how to perform His healing ministry, but trust Him and give thanks and praise to Him in all circumstances, for He alone has all power and desires to receive all the glory.

"See now that I, I am He, And there is no god besides Me; It is I who put to death and give life. I have wounded, and it is I who heal; And there is no one who can deliver from My hand" (Deuteronomy 32:39; see also Psalm 116:15.)

We Don't Ask. Sometimes when we are not healed, it is simply because we fail to consult the Great Physician.

In the Old Testament we read of Asa, who in his thirty-ninth year as king of Judah contracted a disease in his feet. "His disease was severe, yet even in his disease he did not seek the Lord but the physicians. So Asa slept with his fathers" (2 Chronicles 16:12–13).

Mark's Gospel, on the other hand, relates the story of the woman who had hemorrhaged for twelve years. She had spent all she had on doctors, had not been helped but in fact had grown worse.

The woman "after hearing about Jesus, came up in a crowd behind Him, and touched His cloak. For she thought, 'If I just touch His garments, I shall get well.' And immediately the flow of her blood was dried up; and she felt in her body that she was healed of her affliction" (Mark 5:27–29).

God's Natural Laws. Sometimes we don't find healing because we fail to follow God's natural laws, which are as divine as His spiritual laws.

If we do not eat or exercise properly, or otherwise fail to take care of our bodies, we can only expect to reap the consequences of what we sow. (See Galatians 6:7–8.) God expects our obedience to His natural laws so that we will be healthy and thereby honor our body, the temple of the Holy Spirit.

Desire for Sickness. There are some people who through self-pity and a desire for attention or sympathy actually want to be sick. They block God's healing because they disagree with God's will for them to be whole.

(See Matthew 18:19; John 5:6–9; Acts 28:26–27.)

Lack of Knowledge. In the Old Testament God declared, "My people are destroyed for lack of knowledge" (Hosea 4:6). And Solomon the wise tells us how necessary hearing, receiving, and obeying God's Word are to our health:

"My son, give attention to [in other words, obey] my words; Incline your ear to my sayings. Do not let them depart from your sight; Keep them in the midst of your heart. For they are life to those who find them, And health to all their whole body" (Proverbs 4:20–22).

According to Solomon, then, the attentive ear, the steadfast look, and the enshrining heart will bring health to both soul and body.

12.4 TRUST APART FROM HEALING

We must believe God and follow Him whether we are healed or not. Daniel's three friends, Shadrach, Meshach, and Abednego, told the king who had ordered them to serve his gods:

"Our God whom we serve is able to deliver us from the furnace of blazing fire; and He will deliver us out of your hand, O king. But even if He does not, let it be known to you, O king, that we are not going to serve your gods or worship the golden image that you have set up" (Daniel 3:17–18).

Job, for his part, said, "Though He slay me, I will hope in Him" (Job 13:15).

Finally, Oswald Chambers had this to say: " 'It can never be God's will for me to be sick,' one may say. But it was God's will to bruise His own Son. Why then should He not bruise us? What is important is not our idea of what a saint should be, but rather how we are related to Jesus Christ. Are we surrendered to Him whether we are well or afflicted?"

We are to trust God, then; to be persistent and positive; to stand on His Word; and to thank Him in all circumstances. "Pray without ceasing; in everything give thanks; for this is God's will for you in Christ Jesus" (1 Thessalonians 5:17–18).

Our faith is in God, after all, and not in faith. No matter what the outcome, our faith in God must not waver.

God is our healer and His healing ministry is being performed today as we touch the hem of His garment believing for wholeness of spirit, soul and body.

Chapter 13

PRINCIPLES OF GIVING

One of the most frequent difficulties people experience is in the area of finances. Money problems are cited by experts as being one of the leading causes for divorce. Though it sounds glib to mention how materialistic our culture has become, we must nevertheless face the unfortunate fact that we live in a money-oriented society.

For all of us, the pressure is great. Manufacturers and advertising agencies have perfected expert techniques to gather dollars from our pockets. We are pressured on all sides to spend money for things that are supposed to bring us pleasure, joy, and fulfillment; when it is impossible for any *thing* to satisfy our inner emptiness. Only God can do that.

Too many people, Christians included, have not learned the true joy that money can bring—not when it is spent on fleshly desires, but when it is used in God's work to bring comfort and joy to others.

It is important in this section on spiritual maturity, therefore, that we look at principles of giving. Learning to apply these principles can often help us, however slowly, to work our way out of financial difficulties brought on by unbridled spending. For others, it can bring a whole new dimension to their spiritual growth. As one

Church father remarked, giving up our purse to God is like a second conversion.

13.1 WHAT SHOULD WE GIVE?

First, we can give to God by giving Him our heart, our very selves, and we can give to others by considering their interests before our own.

"Do nothing from selfishness or empty conceit, but with humility of mind let each of you regard one another as more important than himself; do not merely look out for your own personal interests, but also for the interests of others" (Philippians 2:3–4).

We can give our time—in prayer and Bible study, in listening, in helping—and use that time wisely. (See Ephesians 5:15–16.)

We can give our talents and abilities, whenever the opportunity arises, to fulfill God's purposes. "As each one has received a special gift, employ it in serving one another, as good stewards of the manifold grace of God" (1 Peter 4:10).

And we can give our resources, the material blessings God has given us, to help others in need.

When the rich man came to Jesus and asked Him what he should do to gain eternal life, Jesus told him: "One thing you lack: go and sell all you possess, and give to the poor, and you shall have treasure in heaven; and come, follow Me" (Mark 10:21).

That man placed greater value on his possessions than on obeying God. He went away grieved, because he would not follow through on a principle he may well have recognized as legitimate: God wants us to give our all to Him. (See Romans 12:8.)

13.2 HOW SHOULD WE GIVE?

We might expect people to be commended for giving generously out of their abundance, but Paul gives us a different kind of example of godly giving in 2 Corinthians 8:1–2. Despite "a great ordeal of affliction" on the part of the churches in Macedonia, "their abundance of joy and their deep poverty overflowed in the wealth of their liberality."

This giving, then, honored by God, came out of affliction and poverty.

In Mark 12:43–44 we read of the poor widow who, "out of her poverty, put in all she owned, all she had to live on."

We are also to give liberally. Paul wrote further about the Macedonian churches: "For I testify that according to their ability, and beyond their ability they gave of their own accord" (2 Corinthians 8:3).

Further, we are to share a common purpose by giving to other members of the Body of Christ. The Macedonian churches begged Paul "with much entreaty for the favor of participation in the support of the saints" (verse 4).

Finally, our giving is to be based on our commitment to God, for "they first gave themselves to the Lord and to us by the will of God" (verse 5).

13.3 WHY SHOULD WE GIVE?

First, giving demonstrates our Christian commitment. "But just as you abound in everything," wrote Paul to the Corinthians, "in faith and utterance and knowledge and in all earnestness and in the love we inspired in you, see that you abound in this gracious work also" (2 Corinthians 8:7).

Giving expresses our love for God and for others. Paul did not command the Corinthians to give, "but as proving through the earnestness of others the sincerity of your love also" (verse 8).

Paul cited Jesus as our greatest example, who "though He was rich, yet for your sake He became poor, that you through His poverty might become rich" (verse 9).

Another important reason to give is simply to meet the needs of others. The abundance of the Christians in Corinth became a supply for the needs of the churches of Macedonia. In the future, the abundance of the Macedonian churches would become a supply for the needs of the Corinthian Christians, "that there may be equality" (verse 14).

Giving to meet someone else's needs now may enable them to meet another's needs—or even our own needs—at some later time.

13.4 GUIDELINES IN GIVING

Paul's exhortation to the Corinthian Christians offers us guidelines to follow in giving.

Be Earnest in Purpose. God had put into Titus' heart an earnestness for giving on behalf of the Corinthian church. "For he not only accepted our appeal," explained Paul, "but being himself very earnest, he has gone to you of his own accord" (2 Corinthians 8:17).

God wants us, too, to be earnest and sincere in our desire to give.

Give with Integrity. We need to be sure we are giving only to an individual, church, or organization that is above reproach.

Paul wrote, "We have sent along with [Titus] the brother whose fame in the things of the gospel has spread through all the churches; and not only this, but he has also been appointed by the churches to travel with us in this gracious work, which is being administered by us for the glory of the Lord Himself, and to show our readiness" (verses 18–19).

Be Honest. We need to administer our gifts honestly and give an accurate accounting for the sake of taxes.

"Taking precaution that no one should discredit us in our administration of this generous gift; for we have regard for what is honorable, not only in the sight of the Lord, but also in the sight of men" (verses 20–21).

Be Proven and Consistent. We are to be faithful in our giving.

"And we have sent with them our brother, whom we have often tested and found diligent in many things, but now even more diligent, because of his great confidence in you" (verse 22).

Be Eager and Ready. Paul knew the readiness of the Christians at Corinth to give, "and your zeal has stirred up most of them" (2 Corinthians 9:2). God will see our eagerness to give, and will channel our efforts and gifts to those who need them. He will also motivate others to give as a result of our joy in giving.

Pray for Others to Have a Heart to Receive. We might pray for those to whom we give, that God will give them a heart to receive our gift.

Paul offers an example in this: "But I have sent the brethren, that our boasting about you may not be made empty in this case, that, as I was saying, you may be prepared; lest if any Macedonians come with me and find you unprepared, we (not to speak of you) should be put to shame by this confidence. So I thought it necessary to urge the brethren that they would go on ahead to you and arrange beforehand your previously promised bountiful gift, that the same might be ready as a bountiful gift, and not affected by covetousness" (verses 3–5).

Give Cheerfully. Most of all, God wants to see us give out of a cheerful heart. "Let each one do just as he has purposed in his heart; not grudgingly or under compulsion; for God loves a cheerful giver" (verse 7).

13.5 PROMISES

God's Word says that if we sow sparingly, we shall also reap sparingly, and if we sow bountifully, we shall reap bountifully.

In the same way, Paul said, "God is able to make *all* grace abound to you, that *always* having *all* sufficiency in *everything*, you may have an *abundance* for *every* good deed" (2 Corinthians 9:8).

What a succession of superlatives!

If, on the other hand, we withhold what is due another person when it is in our power to give, it will result only in want. (See Proverbs 3:27–28, 11:24.)

In Luke 6:38 Jesus said, "Give, and it will be given to you; good measure, pressed down, shaken together, running over, they will pour into your lap. For whatever measure you deal out to others, it will be dealt to you in return."

Running over implies that we will reap even more than we sow.

God has also promised that He who gives us all things will increase our means to give: "Now He who supplies seed to the sower and bread for food, will supply and multiply your seed for sowing and increase the harvest of your righteousness; you will be enriched in everything for all liberality, which through us is producing thanksgiving to God" (2 Corinthians 9:10–11; see also Hosea 10:12).

God will supply our needs to overflowing, creating in us thankful hearts. "For the ministry of this service is not only fully supplying the needs of the saints, but is also overflowing through many thanksgivings to God" (verse 12; see also Philippians 4:19.)

Because our giving shows our obedience to God, it will bring Him glory. "Because of the proof given by this ministry they will glorify God for your obedience to your confession of the gospel of Christ, and for the liberality of your contribution to them and to all (verse 13).

And our giving shows others what God has done in us. "While they also, by prayer on your behalf, yearn for you because of the surpassing grace of God in you" (verse 14).

Paul concludes in verse 15 by thanking God "for His indescribable gift"—our Lord Jesus Christ, the greatest gift we can give to someone else.

III

GETTING TO THE ROOT

Chapter 14

ROOT PROBLEMS

Unconfessed sin produces root problems that hinder God from bringing a person to salvation, filling him with His Holy Spirit, healing him, releasing him from fear, or doing other significant works in his life.

The Bible defines sin as coming short of God's glory (see Romans 3:23). It is anything we allow to come between ourselves and God. When we sin, we rebel against God.

14.1 MAJOR AREAS OF SIN

Our outward actions reveal the condition of our heart, that is to say, if we have unconfessed sin.

Galatians 5:19–21 lists some sin areas: "Now the deeds of the flesh are evident, which are: immorality, impurity, sensuality, idolatry, sorcery, enmities, strife, jealousy, outbursts of anger, disputes, dissensions, factions, envyings, drunkenness, carousings, and things like these, of which I forewarn you just as I have forewarned you that those who practice such things shall not inherit the kingdom of God."

Major areas of sin include the following:

Unforgiveness. When other people offend or hurt us, we need to forgive them; otherwise, God will not forgive us.

"For if you forgive men for their transgressions, your heavenly Father will also forgive you. But if you do not forgive men, then your Father will not forgive your transgressions" (Matthew 6:14–15; see Mark 11:25).

Resentment and Bitterness. We are to be sure that no one sins and comes short of God's grace, so that "no root of bitterness springing up causes trouble" (see Hebrews 12:15). Many will be harmed by a root of bitterness.

Anger. King Solomon cautioned, "Do not be eager in your heart to be angry, For anger resides in the bosom of fools" (Ecclesiastes 7:9).

In the words of James, we are to be "slow to anger; for the anger of man does not achieve the righteousness of God" (James 1:19–20).

(See also Genesis 4:5–7; Leviticus 19:17–18; Proverbs 14:17, 29; 15:18; 19:11, 19; 22:24–25; 29:11; Ephesians 4:31.)

Pride. The Bible says that "God is opposed to the proud, but gives grace to the humble" (1 Peter 5:5; James 4:6). Pride keeps us from depending on God and having a relationship with Him. It says we do not need Him, that we can work out our own lives.

But the Bible warns, "Pride goes before destruction, And a haughty spirit before stumbling" (Proverbs 16:18).

Selfishness. We have a selfish, sinful nature. We want to do things our way. But God wants us to learn to do things His way; to seek to please Him at all times rather than ourselves. Part of pleasing Him means considering others' needs or desires before our own.

"Do nothing from selfishness or empty conceit," Paul wrote to the Philippians, "but with humility of mind let each of you regard one another as more important than himself; do not merely look out for your own personal interests, but also for the interests of others" (Philippians 2:3–4).

Critical or Judgmental Spirit. When we criticize or judge others, we say we are better than they are. This cuts us off from having good relationships.

God is the only one who has a right to judge people. And He balances His judgment with mercy, for He encourages a person at the same time He convicts (or points out areas that need to be changed).

After we have judged others, of course, God usually shows us we have the same or worse faults. The Gospel of John records the incident of the woman caught in adultery. When the scribes and Pharisees brought the woman to Jesus and asked Him what He thought they should do, He responded:

"'He who is without sin among you, let him be the first to throw a stone at her.' And when they heard it, they began to go out one by one, beginning with the older ones, and he was left alone, and the woman, where she had been, in the midst. And straightening up, Jesus said to her, 'Woman, where are they? Did no one condemn you?' And she said, 'No one, Lord.' And Jesus said, 'Neither do I condemn you; go your way; from now on sin no more'" (John 8:7, 9–11).

Even the One who is perfect refused to condemn one who had sinned.

Moral Impurity. We have as much of Sodom and Gomorrah today as in biblical times. Christians who read pornography, watch pornographic movies, commit fornication and adultery, or tell unwholesome jokes, belie the Christian commitment to purity and holiness.

We are not even to allow impure thoughts into our minds. The Bible exhorts us to take "every thought captive to the obedience of Christ" (2 Corinthians 10:5) and to "be transformed by the renewing of your mind" (Romans 12:2). It is sin to entertain impure thoughts. Committing an immoral act is simply the next step.

Moral impurity is rampant around us. We must recognize our sin, and confess and repent of it in order for God to bring us into right standing with Him individually, and even to heal our land.

God holds us accountable for our actions. He expects our obedience to His Word, so we must live accordingly.

14.2 HOW DO WE IDENTIFY AND GET RID OF SIN?

The psalmist prayed, "Search me, O God, and know my heart; Try me and know my anxious thoughts; And see if there be any hurtful way in me, And lead me in the everlasting way" (Psalm 139:23–24).

God will answer when we pray like that, although we may not be prepared for His answer.

We may have something in our lives that displeases God, perhaps a habit. We should get into our prayer closet, getting away from everything else and alone with God. In the quiet moments of our communion with Him, He will begin to point out areas that need work. As God shows us these sins, we may want to write them down on a pad of paper so that we can actually see them in print in front of us.

We can then confess and repent of each of the sins he has pointed out. We must resolve to turn away from them, desiring never to do them again. And God is faithful and just; He forgives us and cleanses us (see 1 John 1:9). We can destroy the paper as a symbolic reminder of the fact that He has already forgiven us.

God requires our obedience. Then and only then we will be released from life-dominating sins. The root of sin will be pulled out of our hearts.

God spoke to His people through the prophet Jeremiah: "Obey My voice, and I will be your God, and you will be My people; and you will walk in all the way which I command you, that it may be well with you" (Jeremiah 7:23).

Sin blocks our communication with God. That is why we sometimes feel when we are praying that we are talking to a wall, or that our prayers are going no higher than the ceiling. Sin has us in its grip; we are bound to it.

But when we confess our sin according to 1 John 1:9, we open up the lines of communication. We can once again enjoy our prayer life and our time with God in His Word. We become spiritually free, and the Holy Spirit produces "love, joy, peace, patience, kindness, goodness, faithfulness, gentleness, self-control; against such things there is no law. Now those who belong to Christ Jesus have crucified the flesh with its passions and desires" (Galatians 5:22–24).

Fruit will grow beautifully in our lives. Our

countenance will reflect the life of Christ, but only when we are released from the power sin has over us. As we confess and repent of sin, we can feel God's love fill us.

14.3 WHAT HAPPENS IF WE DO NOT GET RID OF SIN?

Many people choose not to deal with their sin. They neither want to change nor to obey God. So they live with guilt, which in turn can cause the following:

Mental Problems. These are often problems in living, and not caused by a disease at all. Calling mental problems a disease sometimes relieves a person of his sense of responsibility to confront his problems.

If we view mental and emotional problems as sin, then we need to help the person to recognize his responsibility to confront his sin, that he might be released.

Where these problems persist, a physician should be consulted about possible organic or chemical causes.

Physical Illness. Physical illness can be psychosomatic and caused by unconfessed sin, which leads to organic dysfunction. Author Tim LaHaye reports that 60 to 90 percent of bodily illness is emotionally induced.

The psalmist David wrote, "When I kept silent about my sin, my body wasted away Through my groaning all day long. For day and night Thy hand was heavy upon me; My vitality was drained away as with the fever-heat of summer" (Psalm 32:3–4).

David also wrote, "There is no soundness in my

flesh because of Thine indignation; There is no health in my bones because of my sin. For my iniquities are gone over my head; As a heavy burden they weigh too much for me" (Psalm 38:3–4).

(See also Exodus 15:26; I Corinthians 11:28–30.)

The following illnesses *may* be psychosomatic and caused by unconfessed sin. (But just because a person has one or more of these does not mean he has a root of sin.)

High blood pressure	Heart trouble
Headaches	Ulcers
Colitis	Low back pains
Kidney stones	Gallstones

Inner tension from guilt and blame can disturb the body chemistry. Anger, bitterness, or other sin, if left unattended, may contribute to unbalanced bodily functions and lead to various illnesses.

Separation from God. This is the climax for the person who rebels and refuses to deal with the sin in his life, although none of us wants to be separated from God. "For the wages of sin is death" (Romans 6:23a).

Conversely, a clear conscience and free spirit come in knowing that no one can point a finger at us and say, "You offended me, and you never asked for my forgiveness."

In counseling a person to get rid of sin, we can show him through Scripture that he needs to confess to those he has offended, if possible, and ask their forgiveness. Avoiding details, he should be brief and clear, not involving others. He will want to clear his conscience quickly and then thank God for setting him free.

14.4 HOW DO WE HINDER GOD'S WORK?

The principle of binding and loosing, as mentioned in Matthew 18:18, has not been clearly understood. "Truly I say to you," taught Jesus, "whatever you shall bind on earth shall have been bound in heaven; and whatever you loose on earth shall have been loosed in heaven."

Some have used this verse primarily in "binding" the work of the adversary—that is, Satan. But let us consider other areas that can be affected.

Our ungodly attitudes and actions can bind or hinder our relationships with God and others. When we bind someone, we are in effect causing them to stumble. Jesus said, "It is inevitable that stumbling blocks should come, but woe to him through whom they come!" (Luke 17:1).

The following sins can be binding if not confessed and forsaken:

Unforgiveness	Resentment
Bitterness	Criticism
Wrong judgment	Gossip
Moral impurity	Selfishness
Ungodly relationships	Ungodly involvements

Using unforgiveness as an example, let us see how we can hinder God from working.

Perhaps someone has wronged us by lying about us. We respond not by saying simply that he lied about us; we say that he is a liar—thus labeling and judging him. We continue to distrust him and may encourage others to do so. Others may begin to avoid or scorn him as well, until all humanity is drained from his character and he is "nothing but a liar."

By our unforgiveness, we may actually bind him to the very character traits we would like to see changed, whereas by offering forgiveness we open the way for the Holy Spirit to convict and change him.

How many times should we forgive a person? Scripture indicates no limit to our forgiveness. "Then Peter came and said to Him, 'Lord, how often shall my brother sin against me and I forgive him? Up to seven times?' Jesus said to him, 'I do not say to you, up to seven times, but up to seventy times seven'" (Matthew 18:21–22; see Luke 17:3–4.)

Praying amiss can also hinder God's work in us. If we insist that a particular need be met our way, God may allow us to go our own way to teach us the difference between His will and ours, and that in the end His way is best.

The Old Testament records the desire of the Israelites to go their own way, as well as God's response.

"They quickly forgot His works; They did not wait for His counsel, But craved intensely in the wilderness, And tempted God in the desert. So He gave them their request, But sent a wasting disease among them" (Psalm 106:13–15).

Disobedience to God's Word and praying amiss may be at the root of many of our problems as well.

14.5 WHAT FREES GOD TO WORK?

First, when we ask forgiveness, our heavenly Father will forgive us and release us from the power that sin has over us. "And whenever you stand praying, forgive, if you have anything against anyone; so that your Father also who is in heaven may forgive you your transgressions" (Mark 11:25; see Matthew 5:23–24.)

Second, when we ask God and the offended person to forgive us, we make it possible for God to restore the relationship.

Third, praying with the mind of Christ prevents our praying amiss. Jesus said, "If you abide in Me, and My words abide in you, ask whatever you wish, and it shall be done for you" (John 15:7). Abiding in Christ is the key to praying aright and with His mind. Then we will pray His prayers and accomplish His work.

Only when we are willing to face the root problems in our lives can we begin to help someone else find the path to freedom and wholeness. As counselors, we may see instant changes in those we counsel. But more than likely the path to complete freedom will take time as God produces the changes.

Our satisfaction comes in knowing that one has faced and dealt with the sin in his life and, at that point, found through us the love and healing power of Jesus Christ.

Chapter 15

ANGER AND FEAR

Most sin can be traced to anger or fear, or a combination of both. These may be called the two universal sins.

15.1 HOW ANGER EXPRESSES ITSELF

Anger, a strong feeling of displeasure, expresses itself in several forms, chief of which are bitterness, resentment, and unforgiveness.

Bitterness. Bitterness is detected first in a person's speech and then in his actions and attitudes. If left unchecked by the Holy Spirit, it will settle in the heart, where a root of bitterness will spring up. (See Hebrews 12:15.)

Bitterness leaves a trail of broken relationships and obscures one's vision of life: "But the one who hates his brother is in the darkness and walks in the darkness, and does not know where he is going because the darkness has blinded his eyes" (1 John 2:11).

Bitterness severs one's relationship with God. As a result, we become insensitive to God's Word and will violate it. When we let sin dominate us like this, it becomes difficult to read the Bible and pray. Our spirits are cluttered, for sin has clogged the communication lines between us and God.

Anytime it is difficult to read the Bible or pray,

we should search our hearts and let God point out the sin that is cutting off communication with Him.

A broken relationship with God, moreover, keeps us from growing to spiritual maturity: "If we say that we have fellowship with [God] and yet walk in the darkness, we lie and do not practice the truth; but if we walk in the light as He Himself is in the light, we have fellowship with one another, and the blood of Jesus His Son cleanses us from all sin" (1 John 1:6–7).

Bitterness is one of the greatest tools of destruction the enemy has at his disposal. No Christian can sustain himself in bitterness. The Bible speaks very strongly against this form of anger.

It makes no difference what has caused the bitterness. It must be confessed and forsaken. (See Ephesians 4:31–32; Hebrews 12:15.)

Resentment. This second major variation of anger is a negative hostile feeling usually directed openly at life's difficult circumstances and at God's working in our lives.

Resentment is caused by not getting what we want when we want it. We can be very lustful, selfish people, unwilling to wait for God to fill our needs in His timing. Because we do not get what we want when we want it, we fail to see God's purposes in our waiting, or in satisfying our needs rather than our desires. So we do not trust God. We can then miss His way and the timing of His will for us.

"The mind set on the flesh is hostile toward God; for it does not subject itself to the law of God, for it is not even able to do so; and those who are in the flesh cannot please God" (Romans 8:7–8; see also James 1:6–8; 1 John 2:11.)

God commands us to confess resentment and put it aside so that we might grow into mature Christians. "Therefore, putting aside all malice and all guile and hypocrisy and envy and all slander, like newborn babes, long for the pure milk of the word, that by it you may grow in respect to salvation" (1 Peter 2:1–2).

Unforgiveness. This is the third major expres-. sion of anger. We often overlook Jesus' teaching about continual forgiveness, yet it provides the key to solving many personal problems (review Matthew 18:21–22). We are not to limit how many times we forgive someone.

Unforgiveness is sin against God. If we do not forgive someone who has offended or wronged us, we disobey God and He will not forgive us (see Mark 11:25–26). Nor will our prayers be answered.

Forgiveness begins with a decision, *not* with feelings. We cannot wait for our feelings to change; they may not. We simply have to decide to forgive and act on that decision. We will be miserable until we do. Unforgiveness will not just disappear. We must confront it and resolve it.

If we have unforgiveness, we should take the following steps:

First, we must choose to forgive those who have hurt us. The New Testament says, "Be kind to one another, tender-hearted, forgiving each other, just as God in Christ also has forgiven you" (Ephesians 4:32).

By choosing to forgive, we hinder the work of the enemy. (See 2 Corinthians 2:10–11.)

Second, because unforgiveness is sin, we must confess it to God, and He will cleanse and forgive us. (See Psalm 32:5 and 1 John 1:9).

Third, we need to ask forgiveness of those *we* have wronged. Whether they are readily willing to offer forgiveness or not, our asking for pardon releases us from the wrong we have done so that we can move on to become all that God wants us to be. (See Matthew 5:23–24.)

Fourth, we need to ask God to bless those who have wronged us and pray for those who have mistreated us. (See Luke 6:28.) If it is hard to ask God to bless them, then we have not forgiven them.

Fifth, we also need to bless them by doing something nice for them. Jesus told us to love our enemies and "do good to those who hate you" (Luke 6:27).

Sixth, it makes no difference if the other person is wrong. We are to accept them just as Christ accepts us, treating them with respect and kindness. (See Romans 15:7.)

In asking forgiveness, we are simply obeying God. We are not responsible for whether the person forgives us. We please God by our actions and can ask God to change that person—and us. (See 1 Corinthians 13:7 and Hebrews 12:1.)

Briefly listed below with Scriptures for study are other expressions of anger, all of which God says must be put away.

Malice, Wrath, Clamor, Slander. "But now you also, put them all aside: anger, wrath, malice, slander, and abusive speech from your mouth" (Colossians 3:8; see also Ephesians 4:31 and 1 Peter 2:1).

Envy. "Do not let your heart envy sinners, But live in the fear of the Lord always" (Proverbs 23:17).

Intolerance, Criticism. "Now the people became like those who complain of adversity in the hearing of the Lord; and when the Lord heard it, His anger was kindled, and the fire of the Lord burned among them and consumed some of the outskirts of the camp" (Numbers 11:1).

Revenge. "Never take your own revenge, beloved, but leave room for the wrath of God, for it is written, 'Vengeance is Mine, I will repay,' says the Lord "(Romans 12:19).

Hatred. "If some one says, 'I love God,' and hates his brother, he is a liar; for the one who does not love his brother whom he has seen, cannot love God whom he has not seen" (1 John 4:20–21).

Sedition. "Now Korah . . . took action. . . . And they assembled together against Moses. . . . Then Moses said to Korah, '. . . Therefore you and all your company are gathered together against the Lord' " (Numbers 16:1–11).

Jealousy. "For jealousy enrages a man, And he will not spare in the day of vengeance" (Proverbs 6:34).

Also, "Wrath is fierce and anger is a flood, But who can stand before jealousy?" (Proverbs 27:4).

Attack. "Then Miriam and Aaron spoke against Moses" (Numbers 12:1).

Gossip. "And just as they did not see fit to acknowledge God any longer, God gave them over to a depraved mind, to do those things which are not proper, being filled with all unrighteousness, wickedness, greed, malice; full of envy, murder, strife, deceit, malice; they are *gossips* " (Romans 1:28–29, italics added).

Sarcasm. "Let no unwholesome word proceed from your mouth, but only such a word as is good for edification according to the need of the moment, that it may give grace to those who hear" (Ephesians 4:29; see also Ephesians 5:4.)

15.2 HOW TO DEAL WITH ANGER

We must, first of all, be slow to anger, "for the anger of man does not achieve the righteousness of God"(James 1:20).

Why does God tell us to be slow to anger? What happens when we think twice before getting angry? If God's Spirit dwells in us and controls us, and we are roused to anger, then when we hesitate for a moment, the Holy Spirit can take charge.

It is better yet to "cease from anger, and forsake wrath," the psalmist says. Nor should we fret, because "it leads only to evildoing" (Psalm 37:8).

What happens when we vent our anger? We hurt the person who is the object of our anger. Anger stems from our flesh nature, not from God's Spirit dwelling within us. Therefore, we need to resolve our anger quickly.

"Be angry, and yet do not sin; do not let the sun go down on your anger, and do not give the devil an opportunity" (Ephesians 4:26–27).

God is not giving us license to be angry, but lessons in how to handle anger as it arises. If we become angry, we confess and repent of it immediately. If we have hurt someone, we ask their forgiveness.

Once a word has been spoken, it cannot be taken back. So we need to clear it as quickly as possible to keep the hurt from lingering. So we must quickly take the following steps:

Recognize anger as sin. (See Ephesians 4:30–32.)

Confess our sin to God. (See 1 John 1:9.)

Receive God's forgiveness. (See 1 John 5:14–15.)

Ask God to fill you with His Holy Spirit so that you may truly forgive, too. (See Luke 11:13.)

15.3 HOW FEAR EXPRESSES ITSELF

Fear is an unpleasant and often strong emotion caused by expectation or awareness of danger. Like anger, it expresses itself in many ways.

Doubts. Fear, which is irrational, leads us to doubt. We expect the worst to happen rather than the best. But Jesus said, "If you have faith, and do not doubt, you shall not only do what was done to the fig tree, but even if you say to this mountain, 'Be taken up and cast into the sea,' it shall happen" (Matthew 21:21).

Timidity. Timidity, a form of fear, is not from God. The Bible says, "God has not given us a spirit of timidity, but of power and love and discipline" (2 Timothy 1:7).

Knowing that God has not given us that fear will help us to resist it by exercising the power, love, and discipline (or sound mind) He has given us.

Pride, Haughtiness. If we are proud or haughty, we are afraid to depend on God or on other people. Solomon wrote, "Pride goes before destruction, and a haughty spirit before stumbling" (Proverbs 16:18).

Inferiority. Feelings of inferiority can destroy a person's sense of self-worth, crippling him in his or her interpersonal relationships. He will be afraid to reach out in simple friendliness to others.

Indecision. When God directs us, we are to do as He has said. But when we doubt His direction and vacillate, we become afraid to move out in faith and obedience to His Word.

"But if any of you lacks wisdom, let him ask of God, who gives to all men generously and without reproach, and it will be given to him. But let him ask in faith without any doubting, for the one who doubts is like the surf of the sea driven and tossed by the wind. For let not that man expect that he will receive anything from the Lord, being a double-minded man, unstable in all his ways" (James 1:5–8).

Superstition. This can be an irrational fear of what is unknown or mysterious, especially in connection with religion. When everyone thought that the miracle-worker Jesus was John the Baptist risen from the dead, King Herod (personally responsible for John's murder) was tormented by the fear that "John, whom I beheaded, has risen!" (see Mark 6:16).

Cowardice. In 1 Samuel 17:24 we read, "When all the men of Israel saw the man, they fled from him and were greatly afraid."

Depression. When we are too afraid to face life with its joys and disappointments, we become depressed and cast down, afraid to take a risk and reach out for what God has for us.

Jonah's fear of obeying God by going to Nineveh resulted in severe depression: "And it came about when the sun came up that God appointed a scorching east wind, and the sun beat down on

Jonah's head so that he became faint and begged with all his soul to die, saying, 'Death is better to me than life'" (Jonah 4:8).

Worry. Worry is a major form of fear. It is an emotional sin that plagues the lives of multitudes of Christians. We can believe in Jesus as our Savior and still be guilty of the sin of worry because we do not really *trust* Him.

We worry because we are controlled by feelings. We have not taken control of our mind, dwelling upon the Word of God and having the mind of Christ. We live by our emotions.

Instead of worrying, we must reach out in faith, confess our sin, and cling to God. When we worry about a problem, we are clinging to fear. That only increases the problem. We discredit our faith and especially the God in whom our faith rests.

Sometimes we seem determined to worry. But God says not to do it; it is fear! Worry has no foundation. Throughout the Bible God tells us, "Don't fear. Don't worry. Everything is going to be all right if you put your trust in Me."

In Luke 12:29–32 Jesus said, "Do not seek what you shall eat, and what you shall drink, and do not keep worrying. For all these things the nations of the world eagerly seek; but your Father knows that you need these things. But seek for His kingdom, and these things shall be added to you. Do not be afraid; little flock, for your Father has chosen gladly to give you the kingdom."

We accomplish nothing constructive by worrying. God has never failed to meet our needs. After all, God sees the whole picture. Nothing is too big or too hard for Him. (See Jeremiah 32:17, 27.) We need only to trust Him.

In counseling someone who is worried, ask the following questions:

What is your problem?

What does God want you to do about it according to His Word?

When, where, and how should you begin to overcome the sin of worry?

Anxiety. If we do not get rid of worry, it develops into anxiety, a distress of the mind. Subconscious fears and negative thoughts often cause anxiety. The resulting tension will choke our faith and may even drive us to physical illness.

We cannot deal with anxiety by trying to stop it, or by trying to make ourselves relax. The only effective way to get rid of this distress is to commit ourselves wholly to God. We must call upon Him and know He will preserve us from trouble. (See Psalm 32:7.) As we center our mind on God and His Word, anxiety will go and His perfect peace will come. (See Isaiah 26:3.)

God encourages us to cast all our anxiety on Him because He cares for us (see 1 Peter 5:7). And in Philippians 4:6–7 we are told, "Be anxious for nothing, but in everything by prayer and supplication with thanksgiving let your requests be made known to God. And the peace of God, which surpasses all comprehension, shall guard your hearts and your minds in Christ Jesus."

When we release our requests to God, our fears and anxiety depart and we are filled with His peace.

15.4 HOW TO DEAL WITH FEAR

The Bible makes it clear that fear does not come from God (see 2 Timothy 1:7). And in 1 John 4:18

we see that "there is no fear in love; but perfect love casts out fear, because fear involves punishment, and the one who fears is not perfected in love."

We must seek God's control, then, and His release from fear. The psalmist said, "I sought the Lord, and He answered me, And delivered me from all my fears" (Psalm 34:4).

Finally, most of us would admit that our deepest fears seldom come to pass. We are the ones who produce fear and live with it, because we are afraid that the affairs of our life will somehow move out of our control. Ultimately we are afraid that we will not be able to manipulate events into a pattern that is comfortable for us. So we fear.

For those who truly wish to break lifelong patterns of fear, we must learn to rest in God and trust in His goodness and mercy. Fear is unbelief, and unbelief is sin. As with the sin of anger, God can free us when we confess our fear to Him and trust in His everlasting kindness.

(See Exodus 14:13–14; Psalm 27:1; Isaiah 26:3–4; Matthew 10:26; Hebrews 13:5–6.)

Chapter 16

GUILT AND CONDEMNATION

Guilt can come upon us in one of two forms: as conviction from God for unconfessed sin, or as condemnation from the enemy resulting from real or imagined failures.

God convicts us when we violate His laws. He reveals sin through a guilty conscience, and if we hide it we will not prosper. (See Proverbs 28:13.) When God convicts us of sin and we confess and repent of it, He promises forgiveness, cleansing and a clear conscience. (See 1 John 1:9.) And as we obey God by confessing and forsaking our sin, we will find compassion. (See Proverbs 28:13.)

In Psalm 32:5 David described the result of confessing his sin to God: "I acknowledged my sin to Thee, and my iniquity I did not hide; I said, 'I will confess my transgressions to the Lord'; And Thou didst forgive the guilt of my sin."

On the other hand, Satan condemns us for unconfessed sinful attitudes and actions, or suggests that we contributed to failures in our own life and the lives of others. We can feel condemned in any number of areas: a poor marital relationship, a poor parent/child relationship, a divorce, the death of a spouse or another loved one, financial difficulties, unwise decisions, illness, accidents, negligence, sin.

Jesus said that "the thief comes only to steal,

and kill, and destroy" (John 10:10). Condemnation is one means that the accuser of the brethren uses to destroy us.

Peter warned, "Be of sober spirit, be on the alert. Your adversary, the devil, prowls about like a roaring lion, seeking someone to devour" (1 Peter 5:8).

If we yield to the enemy's tactics, we will be fearful. But if we believe and obey God's Word, we will have boldness to overcome condemnation. We can rest in this promise: "There is therefore now no condemnation for those who are in Christ Jesus" (Romans 8:1). Memorizing and applying that Scripture will serve as a weapon against false accusations against us.

The Bible tells us we are not responsible for the sins of others. "The person who sins will die. The son will not bear the punishment for the father's iniquity, nor will the father bear the punishment for the son's iniquity; the righteousness of the righteous will be upon himself, and the wickedness of the wicked will be upon himself" (Ezekiel 18:20).

Past sins cannot be used against us if we have confessed and forsaken them. We can live with a free and clear conscience, knowing that God will not bring up the past to us again. (See Jeremiah 31:34.) Only Satan will do that, for he accuses us before God "day and night." He is defeated, however, by "the blood of the Lamb and because of the word of their testimony" (see Revelation 12:10–11).

We can also defeat Satan's efforts by submitting to God and resisting him (see James 4:7).

If we are in Christ, we are new creatures, as we have already seen. "old things are passed away;

behold, all things are become new" (2 Corinthians 5:17, KJV).

God will enable us to overcome condemnation: "But thanks be to God who always leads us in His triumph in Christ, and manifests through us the sweet aroma of the knowledge of Him in every place" (2 Corinthians 2:14).

Chapter 17

EMOTIONS AND DEPRESSION

It is estimated that approximately three out of four physical diseases are rooted in mental, emotional, and spiritual problems, rather than in organic difficulties. Here we will consider emotional factors that can lead to depression.

17.1 NEGATIVE EMOTIONS

Three of the most common negative emotions are *fear*—the burden of the future; *anger*—the burden of the present; and *guilt*—the burden of the past.

Fear, anger and guilt—separately or in combination—produce one of the most widespread problems facing people today: depression. Most of those who suffer from depression, which is rooted in the emotions, can trace the cause back to either fear, anger or guilt.

These negative emotions, if unresolved, can also produce psychosomatic responses such as backaches, headaches, sinus conditions, ulcers, nervous ticks, and a myriad of other physical disorders.

17.2 NEED FOR EMOTIONAL HEALING

There are four sources of disturbance that commonly contribute to a need for emotional healing:

Childhood. Failures by our parents often contribute to self-image problems. Other emotional upsets in these formative years can also leave deep scars.

Social Relationships. Peers add to self-image problems leaving wounded memories.

Personal Sin or Unwise Choices. Either of these can lead to unconfessed sin and guilt.

Uncontrolled Circumstances. Mistreatment, being fired from a job, or other seeming injustices may lead to resentment, fear, anger and guilt.

17.3 STEPS TO EMOTIONAL HEALING

First, we must come to trust that the Holy Spirit is by our side. Jesus sent the Helper to be with us at all times. (See John 14:16; and for further instruction on the Holy Spirit, see Chapter 13.)

God also assures us in Romans 8:26–27: "The Spirit also helps our weakness; for we do not know how to pray as we should, but the Spirit Himself intercedes for us with groanings too deep for words; and He who searches the hearts knows what the mind of the Spirit is, because He intercedes for the saints according to the will of God."

Second, we must recognize that it is our response to a problem that creates the need for emotional healing. The psalmist showed us the inner workings of his soul and the way this affected him: "Search me, O God, and know my heart; Try me and know my anxious thoughts; And see if there be any hurtful way in me, And lead me in the everlasting way" (Psalm 139:23–24).

Third, God wants us to release the problem to Him. He has said to cast all our cares and anxieties on Him, because He cares for us. (See 1 Peter 5:7.)

Fourth, once we realize the Holy Spirit is with us, and once we see that the real problem is our response, and are able to release the problem to God, we can believe God will heal us emotionally.

Jesus said, "All things for which you pray and ask, believe that you have received them, and they shall be granted you" (Mark 11:24).

17.4 DEPRESSION

Depression usually occurs when emotions are not healed. It is caused by a sinking of the spirit, evident in a feeling of guilt, hopelessness, or unworthiness. Failure to control or discipline oneself generally leads to depression. It occurs when a person gives in to negative emotions, rather than responding to a problem God's way, which will lead to a positive solution.

A depressed person sometimes lacks motivation even to get up in the morning, much less to accomplish daily responsibilities. Up to a point he feels "down" or discouraged. But once he fails to function normally, he has moved into depression. If the initial symptoms are not resolved, acute depression can lead ultimately to suicidal thoughts.

Depression can be caused by any of the following unresolved root problems:

Unforgiveness	Lingering illness
Negligence	Guilt
Self-pity	Resentment

Stress	Anger
Rejection	Failure
Financial need	Loneliness
Sexual problems	Lack of self-discipline
Lack of a daily schedule	Loss of a loved one
Family conflicts	Fatigue
Bad relationships	Poor self-image
Fear	

God desires that we overcome feelings by responding in a godly way, learning the steps to freedom so that we can say with Paul: "We are afflicted in every way, but not crushed; perplexed, but not despairing; persecuted, but not forsaken; struck down but not destroyed" (2 Corinthians 4:8–9).

What steps can we take to rise above feelings and overcome depression?

The first step is to confess and put away the sin of yielding to feelings and failing to assume responsibilities. (See 1 John 1:9; Romans 6:6–7.)

Second, we need to put God first and obey Him, regardless of how we feel. We must discipline ourselves to follow Him.

Third, we can ask God to search our hearts, as the psalmist did, revealing contributing bad attitudes. (See Psalm 139:23–24.)

Fourth, we can avoid self-pity. Sometimes we think no one else has as much misery as we have. But we are concentrating on ourselves rather than on God and His plan for our lives. One way to avoid feeling sorry for ourselves is to schedule our work, then follow the schedule, not our feelings.

We also need to take the Word of God into our hearts, to fill the void inside us with the sense of God's presence: "Thy word I have treasured in my heart, That I may not sin against Thee" (Psalm 119:11).

In the Old Testament we read that when Elijah wanted to die, an angel of the Lord came to him as he slept and said, "Arise, eat" (1 Kings 19:4–5). That is to say, do not let your feelings master you, contributing to the weakening of your physical body.

Similar practical instructions are found in Matthew 26:46, "Arise, let us be going"; Isaiah 60:1, "Arise, shine"; and John 14:31, "Arise, let us go hence."

We need to persevere in the difficult times, finding the simple task to do that will keep us from wallowing in self-pity.

If depression symptoms persist after taking these steps, physical causes such as chemical imbalance and organic dysfunction must be considered. After prayer, it may be necessary to consult a physician and follow his prescription.

Most depression, however, can be traced to a time of emotional stress. We can encourage anyone who comes to us for counsel that one key to living in God's Kingdom is to bend our wills and do whatever God calls us to do. With this act of obedience will come God's emotional blessings. (See Deuteronomy 28:1–14.)

17.5 SUICIDE

A feeling of hopelessness often leads to acute depression, which in turn may create a desire to take one's life.

When God relented concerning the calamity He had intended to bring on Nineveh, the prophet Jonah gave in to his anger and wanted to die.

"Death is better to me than life," he complained. But God responded, "Do you have good reason to be angry?" (Jonah 4:3–4).

How should *we* respond when someone tells us he or she wants to die?

Usually a person who says he wants to commit suicide is simply reaching out for help and a way out of his depression. We need to show understanding (empathy), compassion (God's love), respect, and sincere concern.

Asking "why" questions will encourage a person to shift the blame. "What" questions will encourage him to be accountable for his actions and find solutions. (See Romans 14:12.) We can patiently, gently encourage a person to talk about his or her problems and feelings, as one would slowly open a pressure release valve. Then we need to help him to see possible solutions and not just the problems.

The following questions will help the counselee to find solutions:

What is wrong?

What happened?

What have you been doing?

What can be done about this situation?

What should your future responses be?

What does God say we must do?

We as counselors must never minimize the counselee's answers. This is vitally important in the listening process.

As the Holy Spirit guides us, we may need to gently remind a believer who contemplates suicide of the words of the New Testament: "Do you not know that you are a temple of God, and that the Spirit of God dwells in you? If any man destroys the temple of God, God will destroy him, for the temple of God is holy, and that is what you are" (1 Corinthians 3:16–17).

Mostly we find that a desperate person needs hope; for "hope does not disappoint us, because God's love has been poured into our hearts through the Holy Spirit which has been given to us" (Romans 5:5).

Regardless of the circumstances—a pregnancy out of marriage, the loss of a loved one, a job termination, or whatever—taking one's life is never the answer. (See Job 5:15–16; Psalm 9:1, 11–12; 34:1, 7; 42:11; John 10:10.)

In severe cases, be sure to refer the counselee to a local pastor or pastoral counselor who is experienced in guiding such hurting individuals through the healing process.

In any case, your willingness to help, to remain in close, friendly contact with a despairing person may be the very lifeline that God uses to draw one up from the darkest pits of the soul into a renewed way of living. Your love and God's everlasting love through you can work miracles.

Chapter 18

GRIEF, DISCOURAGEMENT AND REJECTION

Sometimes the emotions that afflict us are not so severe as depression. Nevertheless, feelings like grief, discouragement, and rejection can temporarily overwhelm a person, robbing them of the abundant life that Jesus Christ promised.

18.1 GRIEF

Grief is an expression of keen mental suffering because of affliction, death, loss or painful regret. Jesus grieved at the death of Lazarus. In a similar way, we as Christians sometimes grieve as an expression of painful sorrow. (See 1 Thessalonians 4:13.)

Grief becomes unbearable when we forego the hope God promises in His Word (such as in Romans 5:5) and move into a state of despair, which is the way of unbelievers without hope.

We must not despair, but trust our God in the midst of pain and sorrow. Because of Him we can have the joy promised in grief (see John 15:11), knowing the blessing that all of God's children receive (see Proverbs 10:22).

God understands grief. But when we prolong it beyond a reasonable amount of time, it can become sin.

18.2 HOW DO WE HELP THOSE WHO GRIEVE?

God is near to comfort those who grieve. At the time of the initial shock of loss, we need to express comfort and compassion. God communicates His own love through us in this way.

"Blessed be the God and Father of our Lord Jesus Christ, the Father of mercies and God of all comfort; who comforts us in all our affliction so that we may be able to comfort those who are in any affliction with the comfort with which we ourselves are comforted by God. For just as the sufferings of Christ are ours in abundance, so also our comfort is abundant through Christ" (2 Corinthians 1:3–5).

Grieving people need to sense the comfort of the Lord Jesus through us. And we can comfort in several ways.

After the initial shock, they may become disoriented because of inevitable changes. We should be sensitive and counsel according to the various stages of grief: anger, fear, depression, unforgiveness, bitterness, resentment, worry, anxieties, guilt, and lack of self-acceptance.

We can encourage a person to hesitate making any hasty or firm decisions during a time of grief because of being unsettled. He needs twelve to eighteen months to adjust. God's timing in all matters is perfect. He has appointed a time for everything: "A time to give birth, and a time to die . . . A time to weep, and a time to laugh; A time to mourn, and a time to dance" (Ecclesiastes 3:2, 4).

God has a plan for each of us, and we may need to help the grieving person discover what that plan is. We will want to encourage him to re-organize his life so that he can find fulfillment and new direction, according to biblical principles and priorities that will please God.

At last that much-needed joy will come into his life.

" 'For I know the plans that I have for you,' declares the Lord, 'plans for welfare and not for calamity to give you a future and a hope. Then you will call upon Me and come and pray to Me, and I will listen to you. And you will seek Me and find Me, when you search for Me with all your heart' " (Jeremiah 29:11–13).

After a spouse goes through a period of grieving, he will realize he must begin to face responsibilities and function again, but now in a single position. In the transition we can help him learn to cope with such matters as insurance, house repairs and maintenance, and finances.

18.3 DISCOURAGEMENT

All of us get discouraged. We lose hope and courage. Our hearts grow weary.

The root cause of discouragement is that we lower our shield of faith (see Ephesians 6:16), allowing the fiery darts of fear, unbelief, bitterness, and self-pity to defeat us.

Discouragement is one of the enemy's most effective weapons against us. He thrives on tearing us down. (See Revelation 12:10.) But God builds us up, even in chastisement.

The first state of discouragement is mild. Then it becomes stronger until it disables us and we become deeply depressed.

18.4 HOW DO WE OVERCOME DISCOURAGEMENT?

We need to get rid of any guilt by repentance and confession.

We also must deal with discouragement by "keeping faith and a good conscience" (1 Timothy 1:19). In taking up the shield of faith, we "extinguish all the flaming missiles of the evil one" (see Ephesians 6:16).

The battle against discouragement and defeat is won or lost in the mind. God has given us authority over the enemy's lies, and we are to counter those lies with God's truth. Consider some of the following:

Lie: God has left you.

Truth: "I will never leave thee, nor forsake thee" (Hebrews 13:5, KJV).

Lie: No good will come; it will never work out.

Truth: "All things work together for good to them that love God" (Romans 8:28, KJV).

Lie: People hurt you.

Truth: "We wrestle not against flesh and blood, but against . . . spiritual wickedness" (Ephesians 6:12, KJV).

Lie: God is punishing you.

Truth: "For those the Lord loves He disciplines" (Hebrews 12:6). (Punishment from the enemy tears us down, but discipline from the Lord corrects and builds us up.)

Lie: You have no strength; you can't do anything.

Truth: "My strength is made perfect in weakness" (2 Corinthians 12:9, KJV), and, "I can do all things through Him who strengthens me" (Philippians 4:13).

We need to tell God we will believe and accept His truth and not the enemy's lies. We never have to accept anything that will separate us from a whole relationship with Jesus Christ, and believing lies over God's truth will do that.

Second, David encouraged himself in the Lord (1 Samuel 30:6b), and we can do the same. (See also Matthew 26:46.)

Some of the greatest encouragement comes through reading the Psalms. By delighting in God's Word and meditating on it day and night, especially as we go to sleep, we will strengthen our hearts.

Too, we should choose our companions wisely—those who will encourage us, not discourage us; those who are positive, not negative or fearful.

"Who is the man that is afraid and fainthearted? Let him depart and return to his house, so that he might not make his brothers' hearts melt like his heart"(Deuteronomy 20:8.)

As long as we keep our eyes on God, we cannot lose heart and become discouraged for long. God takes our discouragement and turns it around for our good.

18.5 REJECTION

Rejection is that feeling of not being accepted—being cast aside, overlooked, forsaken—or the feeling that one has failed to measure up to expected standards.

Rejection comes in relationships between:

Husbands and Wives. A wife often feels rejected by her husband, especially if he is not fulfilling his role and encouraging her and helping to build up her self-esteem. Divorce brings with it a deep sense of rejection in both mates.

Peers. We may be rejected by other members of the Body of Christ, fellow employees, schoolmates, and social contacts.

Employers and Employees. We sense rejection when we are treated less than equal to other employees.

Parents and Children. A child may feel rejected for not being the sex his parents wanted, or even for coming along unexpectedly, or perhaps at what seemed to the parents an inconvenient time.

Brothers and Sisters. Sibling rivalry etches deep scars of rejection in more sensitive children. But these scars can be healed.

God and Men. We cry out, "God, where are You? Have You left Me?" Even Jesus felt forsaken by the Father as He hung on the cross bearing our sins.

We can also reject ourselves and displease God when we do not love ourselves. Needed is not a prideful love. We need to love ourselves because God created us.

But God has promised never to forsake us and never to cast out or reject the one who comes to Him (see John 6:37).

We experience rejection if our talents are ignored or someone thinks we do not have a good personality. Or our achievements may appear less than someone else's. We may feel rejected on our job if we are passed over for a promotion, or among friends if our beliefs differ from theirs.

Christ provides the ultimate example of rejection. "He was despised and forsaken of men, a man of sorrows, and acquainted with grief; and like one from whom men hide their face, He was despised, and we did not esteem Him" (Isaiah 53:3).

18.6 HOW DO WE HELP THOSE WHO FEEL REJECTED?

Jesus took our rejection on Himself. He paid the price for our total healing at Calvary. "Surely our griefs He Himself bore, and our sorrows He carried; Yet we ourselves esteemed Him stricken, Smitten of God, and afflicted" (Isaiah 53:4).

Because of Jesus' sacrifice, God loves us and will *never* forsake us. (See Hebrews 13:5.)

We need to forgive ourselves and others. If we do not, we break our relationship with God and with those we cannot forgive, even when they reject us. "Be kind to one another, tender-hearted, forgiving each other, just as God in Christ also has forgiven you" (Ephesians 4:32; see also Matthew 6:14–15.)

We must release to God the individuals we feel have rejected us. Otherwise, we may try to pay them back by rejecting or hurting them. And God's Word says, "Never take your own revenge, beloved, but leave room for the wrath of God, for it is written, 'Vengeance is Mine, I will repay,' says the Lord" (Romans 12:19).

Likewise, Jesus commanded us to love our enemies and do good to those who hate us. (See Luke 6:27.)

It is important to keep on loving as Christ did, unconditionally and without limit, through the rejection we suffer. The love of God communicated through us will dispel the hurt of rejection.

Chapter 19

ALCOHOLISM AND DRUG ABUSE

A person with an alcohol or drug abuse problem has come under the influence and control of a mind stimulant or depressant that affects his spiritual, physical, emotional, and mental functions. The problem is caused by a person's seeking fulfillment, an escape from emptiness, and by his lack of purpose and self-control. It is sin, not a sickness, but it can lead to sickness.

Alcohol and drug abuse result in an inability to cope with daily living. To overcome the problem, a person must realize he needs to change and believe that he can be released.

Abuse habits produce life-dominating problems. The individual is responsible before God and cannot blame another person or his circumstances for the choice he has made. Just because one's father or mother is an alcoholic does not force him to become one.

The Bible names alcoholism as a sin: "Now the deeds of the flesh are evident, which are: immorality, impurity, sensuality, idolatry, sorcery, enmities, strife, jealousy, outbursts of anger, disputes, dissensions, factions, envyings, drunkenness, carousings, and things like these, of which I forewarn you just as I have forewarned you that those who practice such things shall not inherit the kingdom of God" (Galatians 5:19–21).

(See also Leviticus 10:9; Proverbs 20:1; 23:29–35; 31:4–6; Isaiah 22:12–13; 28:7; Romans 13:13; 1 Corinthians 6:12; Ephesians 5:18; 1 Peter 4:3–5.)

Alcoholism and drug abuse may well lead to other problems. If someone is an alcoholic, their spouse, children, other family members, friends, and fellow workers all suffer, too. The problem may even lead to stealing, lying, or other forms of dishonesty in the effort to support or cover up the sin.

We might broaden this area of substance abuse to include overeating, smoking, and other abuses of our bodies that are an abomination to God. Many things defile the temple of the Holy Spirit. (See Isaiah 5:11; Luke 21:34; 1 Corinthians 6:9–10; Proverbs 23:20–21.)

19.1 STEPS TO OVERCOMING ALCOHOLISM AND DRUG ABUSE

A person must first submit his life to Christ's control. Herein lies his only hope for release and salvation. At the same time, he must recognize his sin, confess it, and forsake it. He can then realize the promise of being set free.

"Do not be deceived; . . . drunkards . . . shall [not] inherit the kingdom of God. And such were some of you; but you were washed, but you were sanctified, but you were justified in the name of the Lord Jesus Christ, and in the Spirit of our God" (1 Corinthians 6:9–11).

He then needs to give all his sinful desires to God, taking authority over those desires. (See Matthew 10:1; 16:19; 28:18; Luke 9:1), and trust God to release him. "If therefore the Son shall make you free, you shall be free indeed" (John 8:36).

Once a person is free of sin, no matter what it is, he will need to fill that void with Jesus Christ and His Spirit. As Paul admonishes us, "And do not get drunk with wine, for that is dissipation, but be filled with the Spirit" (Ephesians 5:18).

Self-control is a fruit of being filled with the Holy Spirit and it is the key to overcoming these sin areas.

The first step in learning self-control is to put off the old nature of alcoholism, drug abuse, or gluttony and put on the new nature, as Paul points out:

"That, in reference to your former manner of life, you lay aside the old self, which is being corrupted in accordance with the lusts of deceit, and that you be renewed in the spirit of your mind, and put on the new self, which in the likeness of God has been created in righteousness and holiness of the truth" (Ephesians 4:22–24; see also 1 Corinthians 3:16–17 and 6:19–20).

Second, the person must leave his old friends and the old lifestyle to allow God's Spirit to change him. We are not to be deceived, the New Testament says, "Bad company corrupts good morals" (1 Corinthians 15:33).

Instead, the person should seek out godly friends and fellowship so he can grow as a Christian. Godly friends will provide strength and encouragement to keep him from falling back into sin.

Third, regular Bible study and unceasing communion with God will help fill the inner void. As Jesus told His followers, "Pray that you may not enter into temptation" (Luke 22:40).

Finally, the one who is released from substance abuse should give thanks and praise to God who has set him free. (See 2 Corinthians 2:14.)

As a counselor, you must recognize that release will come only when individuals are ready and willing to change. If they do not see themselves as needing to change, you present the way toward freedom. In due time they will seek to change and submit their lives to Christ. Your faithful prayers will bring this to pass.

Chapter 20

SEXUAL SIN ADULTERY, FORNICATION, HOMOSEXUALITY

Among the sexual transgressions discussed in the Bible, adultery, fornication, and homosexuality are probably the most prevalent today.

20.1 ADULTERY AND FORNICATION

Adultery means to engage in sexual relations with someone other than one's lawful spouse. An unmarried person commits fornication when he or she engages in sexual relations with someone else, whether married or unmarried.

According to the Bible, those who commit adultery or fornication will not enter heaven. They will be separated eternally from God:

"Know ye not that the unrighteous shall not inherit the kingdom of God? Be not deceived: neither fornicators, nor idolaters, nor adulterers, nor effeminate, nor abusers of themselves with mankind, Nor thieves, nor covetous, nor drunkards, nor revilers, nor extortioners, shall inherit the kingdom of God" (1 Corinthians 6:9–10, KJV; see also Galatians 5:19–21).

God commands, "You shall not commit adultery" (Exodus 20:14). Jesus took the command even further: "You have heard that it was said, 'You shall not commit adultery'; but I say to you, that every one who looks on a woman to lust for

her has committed adultery with her in his heart"
(Matthew 5:27–28).

We are to take some strict measures, therefore,
to protect ourselves from falling to this temptation. One measure is to do as Job did: "I have
made a covenant with my eyes; How then could I
gaze at a virgin?" (Job 31:1). That is, he did not
allow his eyes—or his thoughts—to carry him
into sin.

Too, a person would be wise to follow Paul's
injunction: "Now concerning the things about
which you wrote, it is good for a man not to touch
a woman" (1 Corinthians 7:1).

What should our response be to someone, in
particular, a spouse, who commits adultery?

God commanded Hosea to receive his unfaithful wife after she had committed adultery. (See
Hosea 3:1–3.)

God requires our obedience to His command
not to commit adultery. Confessing and forsaking
the sin will restore one's relationship to God. And
forgiveness will restore one's relationship to
others.

(See Chapter 22 for a more complete discussion
about counseling marital difficulties.)

20.2 HOMOSEXUALITY

Homosexuality, a sexual lusting relationship
between two persons of the same sex, is a
behavioral sin that creates tremendous emotional
and social problems and can lead to death. Homosexual males are often referred to as gays, and
females as lesbians.

Homosexuality was a life-dominating sin as far
back as the Old Testament. Today it has become

increasingly widespread and accepted by our society as well.

What Does the Bible Say? The Bible calls homosexuality an abomination. (See Leviticus 18:22.) Those who practice it will not inherit the Kingdom of God. (See 1 Corinthians 6:9–10.)

Homosexuals rebel against God's original plan for one man and one woman to join together for life, to establish the home and the priesthood in the home, and to be fruitful and multiply. (See Genesis 1:27–28.) Homosexuality violates God's creative plan. He did not desire two men or two women to live together in a marriage relationship.

Even some who profess to be Christians claim that homosexuality is all right. They say, "God is a forgiving God, and He wants me to feel good." But that is heresy and a contradiction of God's Word.

Reaching these people with the truth is very difficult. Unless they want to be set free, we can do little but explain the Scriptures to them, pray, and extend God's love. God loves homosexuals very much, but He does not tolerate their sin.

When a person is open to hearing God's Word, certain Scriptures might be helpful in showing them that homosexuality is a sin.

One of the strongest is in Romans: "Therefore God gave them over in the lusts of their hearts to impurity, that their bodies might be dishonored among them. . . . God gave them over to degrading passions; for their women exchanged the natural function for that which is unnatural, and in the same way also the men abandoned the natural function of the woman and burned in their desire towards one another, men with men committing indecent acts and receiving in their own persons the due penalty of their error. And, although they know the ordinance of God, that those who practice such things are worthy of death, they not only do the same, but also give hearty approval to those who practice them" (Romans 1:24, 26–27, 32).

(See also Genesis 19:5; Leviticus 20:13; Deuteronomy 23:17–18; Judges 19:22; 1 Kings 14:24; 1 Kings 15:12; 1 Kings 22:46; 2 Kings 23:7; Romans 6:11–14, 22; Ephesians 5:5; 1 Timothy 1:9–10.)

Characteristics of the Homosexual. A homosexual practices the act or fantasizes about it. Fantasizing is as sinful as committing the act.

He may look normal in appearance, or variant, depending on role.

He most often has a poor self-image and hates himself.

He may be sadistic in nature and have unnatural sex desires.

He may be convinced he was born a homosexual and that there is no way out.

He is deceived and, like every human being at one time, a slave to sin.

He may manipulate people, trying to make others feel that what he is doing is acceptable.

He may be promiscuous, moving from one relationship to another.

He may be manic depressive.

He may be schizophrenic.

He may be addicted to alcohol/drugs.

How Do We Help the Homosexual? When someone desires to be released, we must point that person to the cross of Christ. Also, we can stress that they must acknowledge homosexual behavior as sin, and confess it and repent of it in our presence and before God.

The person needs to ask God to help him break the habit pattern that leads to the sin. Change comes when we see the pattern and break it by deliberately engaging in a different pattern that can lead away from the act. The old sinful pattern must be broken and replaced by the new godly one. For the Bible says that if God's Son makes us free, "We will be free indeed" (see John 8:36). In some cases, the path to freedom includes deliverance. (See Chapter 33.)

Primarily, one who has been released from homosexuality must avoid all former homosexual friends and places where these people gather.

Second, he should begin to relate to people who have never had the problem or have completely come out of this lifestyle and are committed to and involved with Christ and His Church. Through strong, godly relationships he can overcome temptations in this sin area. (See Proverbs 13:20 and Hebrews 10:23–25.)

He also needs to cultivate wholesome thought patterns and never permit his mind to visualize deviant or immoral behavior. Scripture says we are to be transformed or changed by the renewing of our mind (see Romans 12:1–2).

How does one cultivate healthy thought patterns? Again: "Whatever is true, whatever is honorable, whatever is right, whatever is pure, whatever is lovely, whatever is of good repute, if there is any excellence and if anything worthy of praise, let your mind dwell on these things" (Philippians 4:8).

Finally, the person who has been released from

homosexuality must start living a disciplined life. He may think that to leave his old lifestyle is the hardest thing he has ever done. However, Jesus promised, "With men it is impossible, but not with God; for all things are possible with God" (Mark 10:27).

Without hope, living a disciplined life would be unattainable. But "hope does not disappoint, because the love of God has been poured out within our hearts through the Holy Spirit who was given to us" (Romans 5:5; see also 1 Corinthians 9:24–27.)

Our hope comes from God's Word, which says we are to walk by the Spirit, and not by the desires of the flesh. (See Galatians 5:16.) The fruit or evidence of the Spirit in a believer's life is love, joy, peace, patience, kindness, goodness, faithfulness, gentleness, and most particularly self-control (see Galatians 5:22–23).

To live above sin, we need to saturate ourselves with God's Word through study, handling the Scriptures properly and with accuracy. (See 2 Timothy 2:15).

"All Scripture is inspired by God and profitable for teaching, for reproof, for correction, for training in righteousness; that the man of God may be adequate, equipped for every good work" (2 Timothy 3:16–17).

Bible study, prayer, and praise will lead a person to a life full of overcoming power and good works, produced by a godly faith (see James 2:18) and a disciplined life committed to Christ (see Romans 6:5–23).

IV

ONE
FLESH

Marriage

The Wife's Role

The Husband's Role

Building a Godly Home

Divorce and Remarriage

Chapter 21

MARRIAGE

If the Body of Christ contains a weakness, it lies in the family. Nearly one out of two marriages among non-Christians ends in divorce. And sadly, the divorce rate among Christians nearly parallels that figure.

In counseling someone concerning marital problems, we should enter into it cautiously and preferably with both marriage partners present. There are problems on both sides of every marriage relationship. We cannot make decisions based only on one partner's view of the problems. We also have to guard against counseling out of our personal feelings. Most important, our counsel must always line up with the Word of God.

Our main concern in all marital difficulties is reconciliation and restoration. No matter what the problem—including adultery, wife abuse, and child abuse—we must not counsel anyone hastily to leave a spouse. That is not our choice.

Instead, we need to refer the person to in-depth counseling and seek his or her emotional health and wholeness. God heals; He does not tear apart. We need to give Him a chance.

Because marriage is such a complex area in which to counsel, the scriptural applications set forth here may differ from those that others have presented.

21.1 MARRIAGE IS A COVENANT RELATIONSHIP

God has never broken His covenant with His chosen people, the Jews, and He never will. It is a binding agreement between God and the Jews. That is the same kind of covenant relationship God expects a husband and wife to have.

If we break our marriage covenant, moreover, our prayers may not be answered: "Yet you say, 'For what reason [does God not regard your offering]?' Because the Lord has been a witness between you and the wife of your youth, against whom you have dealt treacherously, though she is your companion and your wife by covenant" (Malachi 2:14).

A covenant is a binding promise made to God. When we treat that commitment lightly, it breeds rebellion. And that rebellion appears in marriage. The vow husbands and wives make to each other is a covenant, a commitment, and not to be taken lightly.

21.2 A GOD'S-EYE VIEW

God designed marriage from the beginning of time. He created the man, Adam, first.

"Then the Lord God said, 'It is not good for the man to be alone; I will make him a helper suitable for him.' So the Lord God caused a deep sleep to fall upon the man, and he slept; then He took one of his ribs, and closed up the flesh at that place. And the Lord God fashioned into a woman the rib which He had taken from the man, and brought her to the man. And the man said, 'This is now bone of my bones, And flesh of my flesh; She shall be called Woman, Because she was taken out of

Man.' For this cause a man shall leave his father and his mother, and shall cleave to his wife; and they shall become one flesh" (Genesis 2:18, 21–24).

God took a rib out of man's side, which says that a woman stands equal by her husband's side as his helpmeet—not above or below him, but by his side. Let's examine the dynamics of this relationship.

Leaving. What does it mean to leave one's parents? It means to establish an adult relationship with our parents. We are no longer children; we are a new family unit created by God. We remain sons or daughters, but as adults.

To leave one's parents also means that we become more concerned about our mate's ideas, opinions, and practices than about our parents'. Our allegiance changes. The new family in Christ becomes a greater priority than our old family. Parents must cut the apron strings or coattails, being careful to stay out of the new marriage relationship.

Something changes in our emotions, too. We no longer depend primarily on our parents for affection, approval, assistance, and counsel. Our dependence now is on God and the communication with our mate. A separation has been made.

Separation from parents is essential to a biblical marriage in other ways as well. We must separate from the bad experiences of the past, resolving wrong attitudes toward our parents. If a son or daughter has resentment, bitterness, or unforgiveness toward their parents, they need to settle it before marriage so they do not carry those negative emotions into the new relationship. Those emotions can cause stress between a husband and wife.

Sometimes we must learn to leave behind our parents' standards and not try to change our mate because of our parents' desires. Parents often have an image of what their son or daughter's mate should be. They want to fit him or her into their mold, while God wants to fit both mates into His mold.

Parents need to release their children and mates to God, even when they see things that are not pleasing to them. Parents are to give counsel and be in agreement prior to marriage, but whatever is left unfinished must be released to God for Him to accomplish.

A couple must make the husband-wife relationship top priority above any other human relationship. No longer do a man and woman return to their old friends and treat them better than they treat their mate. No longer do they let time with their parents take precedence over time with their mate. Every other relationship becomes secondary. It is God and the husband and wife; the relationship they have with Him and with one another is now the priority.

Cleaving. What does it mean to cleave to one another through marriage? In cleaving, we cling to one another; we are in the process of becoming one.

We vow to be faithful to one another until death. Today that old vow, "Till death do us part," may not be significant to some. Some may say, "The marriage is dead, so I'm getting out." But marriage is a commitment two people make not only to one another but also before God.

Cleaving means we make a deliberate choice. We are going to stand on that choice and participate in it. Cleaving is a matter of obedience, not convenience. Too many marriages are formed and lived out of convenience. Yet we are trying to develop something stronger than that—obedience. For we must base our marriages upon commitment, not feelings.

In cleaving we are willing and determined to work at the relationship; to work to keep the marriage together. This includes working at attitudes.

Some say marriage is a fifty-fifty relationship. In the principle of sowing and reaping, however, we are asked to give one hundred percent to one another, expecting nothing in return. By our attitude and our obedience to God's Word, we will reap a blessing. Both spouses must learn to love and give and give—one hundred percent.

This takes discipline and dying to self, a yielding of our rights to God, so that we can continue relating to one another when our feelings have been hurt by petty misunderstandings. As problems arise, each partner should say to God, "Change me," instead of saying, "Change my mate."

Cleaving means we are to be joined to one another in sickness and health, poverty and wealth, pleasure and pain, joy and sorrow, good times and bad, agreements and disagreements. We face problems together, discuss them, seek God's help, and resolve them because there is no way out. We enfold the marriage into God's Word, joining the two together, fitting the marriage into the Bible. When problems arise, we work them out instead of running from them. No battle has ever been won by running.

Committed to one another for life, a husband and wife must remember that what God has put together, no one is to tear apart.

Becoming One. What does it mean to be one flesh through marriage?

Within the bounds of marriage is a physical or sexual union, which is good and beautiful and holy. This sexual union also has a spiritual aspect, however, that is often overlooked. So it is that many husbands and wives miss one of the greatest blessings God has for them.

Becoming one flesh means achieving total intimacy and deep unity. We are transparent with one another. God wants us to communicate and be intimate with our mate. That takes honesty and a willingness to bare one's soul.

Becoming one means we share everything, including our bodies, possessions, insights, ideas, abilities, problems, successes, sufferings, and failures. Again, transparency is essential.

We are as concerned about the other person's needs as we are about our own. The Bible says we are to regard others as better than ourselves (see Philippians 2:3–4). This principle certainly holds true for marriage, in which husband and wife are not to live by feelings. They should never pay back evil for evil or insult for insult (see Romans 12:17).

Even differences need not hinder marital unity. For example, the arrival of children may reveal a conflict regarding discipline. One parent may be a strong disciplinarian and the other not as strong. God can bring a balance to that difference, if we let Him. Differences should provide an opportunity to express love, and to grow and stretch in the Lord Jesus.

Breaking Up. What can destroy marital unity? Sin is the only force that can destroy a marriage.

Many sins affect the marriage relationship, and these are at the root of adultery and desertion. There is selfishness (probably the major reason), pride, bitterness, unforgiveness, resentment, ingratitude, unwholesome speech, neglect, cruelty, impatience, harshness, and insensitivity.

The writer of Hebrews admonishes us to "let marriage be held in honor among all" (13:4).

God created marriage from the very beginning. It is not something we enter into based on feelings or out of convenience. We enter marriage out of obedience to God. He created man and woman and blessed them (see Genesis 1:27–28). To honor marriage is to honor God. (See Matthew 19:5; Mark 10:7–8; Ephesians 5:31.)

21.3 PERMANENCE

Too many people enter marriage with the idea that if it does not work out, they can divorce their spouse and marry someone else. They are starting out in violation of God's Word.

"But to the married I give instructions," wrote the apostle Paul, "not I, but the Lord, that the wife should not leave her husband (but if she does leave, let her remain unmarried, or else be reconciled to her husband), and that the husband should not send his wife away" (1 Corinthians 7:10–11).

That indicates the permanence God intended.

Paul went on to write: "But to the rest I say, not the Lord, that if any brother has a wife who is an unbeliever, and she consents to live with him, let him not send her away. And a woman who has an unbelieving husband, and he consents to live with her, let her not send her husband away. For the unbelieving husband is sanctified through his wife, and the unbelieving wife is sanctified through her believing husband; for otherwise your children are unclean, but now they are holy" (1 Corinthians 7:12–14).

When there is an unequally yoked marriage because one spouse has come to Christ, there is no excuse for breaking up the relationship if the unbeliever desires to stay.

The Bible instructs us not to marry an unbeliever: "Do not be bound together [mismated] with unbelievers; for what partnership have righteousness and lawlessness, or what fellowship has light with darkness?" (2 Corinthians 6:14).

Those who marry unbelievers violate God's Word, and often pay the price.

If a marriage, either by choice or circumstances, is an unequal relationship, both partners may be committed to one another, but only one is committed to God. God allows such a partnership because He lets us choose to go our own way, but it is neither His desire nor His best for us.

Divorce is not God's will, or an option. God's heart is for a permanent marriage relationship to be established. But because of our hardness of hearts, He permits divorce, as Jesus told the Pharisees: "Because of your hardness of heart, Moses permitted you to divorce your wives; but from the beginning it has not been this way" (Matthew 19:7–8).

Jesus also said, "Every one who divorces his wife and marries another commits adultery; and he who marries one who is divorced from a husband commits adultery" (Luke 16:18).

We will see in the next chapter that God does allow divorce on certain grounds. But He permits it only because of the hardness of our hearts. It is neither His will nor an option that we may offer as Christian counselors.

Chapter 22

THE WIFE'S ROLE

What does the Bible say about the wife's role in marriage? What problems does she face? How has the world shaped her? What keeps her from being the woman God wants her to be in a marriage relationship?

The one quality a woman needs to become the wife God designed her to be is yieldedness to Him and to her husband. It may be her heart's desire to fit into her husband's plans. But only when a woman yields to God and His purposes and ways has she taken the first step to a happy, fulfilled relationship with her husband.

22.1 A HELPER FOR MAN

The Bible states clearly why God created woman: "Then the Lord God said, 'It is not good for the man to be alone; I will make a helper suitable for him'" (Genesis 2:18).

God knew that man needed a helper, so He created woman to be the perfect, "suitable" complement to him. She is a companion in labor who gives assistance, relief, or aid in the home, family, or ministry. Conflict arises when she tries to do something else. As many women are discovering today, serious personal and marital problems result when they work in a profession that requires a man's aggressive nature.

We have to accept, primarily, that God gave certain duties to a man and certain duties to a woman.

"And God created man in His own image, in the image of God He created him; male and female He created them. And God blessed them; and God said to them, 'Be fruitful and multiply, and fill the earth, and subdue it; and rule over the fish of the sea and over the birds of the sky, and over every living thing that moves on the earth'" (Genesis 1:27–28).

God has called women to be fruitful and multiply. That means more than having children, which is very important. Added to the fruit of a woman's body should be the fruit of the Spirit. Leading others to Christ, and encouraging and teaching other believers to bear spiritual fruit, are other facets of being fruitful and multiplying.

God has also called women to take dominion over the earth and over the enemy. Satan has too much freedom in marriages and in homes today. He has this freedom in part because we fail to take dominion over him.

We need, then, to understand the works of the enemy, the fiery darts and strongholds or fortresses he has built in our lives. Each of us has a stronghold where at one time we gave place to the enemy. And whenever we are at a weak point, he will throw his fiery darts into that stronghold.

As praying wives and mothers, women must ask God for wisdom to know what the weak places are, so they may function in the simple duty He has given them—to take dominion over the enemy and subdue him.

It is important to know also that God established an authority structure in marriage. We may not like it, but if we believe that God is perfect, and if we would know His perfect order, then we must accept what His Word teaches, such as in 1 Corinthians 11:3: "But I want you to understand that Christ is the head of every man, and the man is the head of a woman, and God is the head of Christ."

Is a woman to obey her husband? What does the Bible say? If the Bible says it, we are to do it. If we do not obey, we rebel, and "rebellion is as the sin of witchcraft" (1 Samuel 15:23, KJV).

It is serious to rebel against God's Word. A woman may not like what it says, but she must do what it says: "Wives, be subject to your own husbands, as to the Lord" (Ephesians 5:22).

In this, though, it is important to understand that God's purposes are not harsh or unreasonable, but orderly and wise. For when a woman obeys God's authority structure in marriage, she can exercise true, godly authority and power.

22.2 POWER OF THE WIFE

As a man has the power of position, so the woman has the power of influence, which she can use to build up or tear down. So much of what happens in a marriage depends on a woman. By her heart attitude, she can make or break her home, her marriage, her husband, her children.

"An excellent wife is the crown of her husband," wrote Solomon, "but she who shames him is as rottenness in his bones" (Proverbs 12:4). Similarly, "The wise woman builds her house, But the foolish tears it down with her own hands" (Proverbs 14:1).

It truly is up to the woman. How does she

spend her time? What does she do with her life? How much is she willing to relinquish in order for her marriage and her home to be what God desires it to be?

God has given the woman a powerful tool—her great influence. How is she going to use it? Is she going to use it for good, to glorify God, or for destruction? The choice is hers.

22.3 THE SUBMISSIVE WIFE

Submission is not something you do; rather, it is an attitude of the heart. When we come to Christ, we come by faith, and our faith produces works. Our hearts are changed, and out of that change come works or fruit.

Likewise in the marriage relationship the heart must be changed, and the works will follow. Works without a changed heart will produce no power in either the wife or husband. With a changed heart, however, the wife's works will effect a change in her husband, because her works will then be motivated by the Holy Spirit, not by the flesh.

In short, the wife must change in order for the husband to change. Instead of asking God to change their husbands, wives should ask, "Lord, change me."

Two passages in 1 Peter point out the attitudes a wife needs to develop.

"Servants, be submissive to your masters with all respect, not only to those who are good and gentle, but also to those who are unreasonable. For this finds favor, if for the sake of conscience toward God a man bears up under sorrows when suffering unjustly. For what credit is there if, when you sin and are harshly treated, you endure it with patience? But if, when you do what is right and suffer for it you patiently endure it, this finds favor with God. For you have been called for this purpose, since Christ also suffered for you, leaving you an example for you to follow in His steps" (1 Peter 2:18–21).

What is His purpose but that we be formed into the image of Jesus Christ? If dying to self was enough for Christ, it is enough for us. Reflecting the same wisdom Peter showed, Paul wrote to the Philippians, saying that Jesus "did not regard equality with God a thing to be grasped, but emptied Himself" (see Philippians 2:5–8).

In every godly relationship, we have to die to our own rights, to be crucified with Christ, to develop the heart attitude of a bondservant that Christ had. This will enable us when we are "reviled," or abused verbally, not to retaliate or "revile in return" (see 1 Peter 2:23). Christ did not. Nor did He regard His equality with God "a thing to be grasped."

God's Word says that a woman is equal with her husband. Is she going to grasp at that? The Christlike attitude is not to grasp at it, but to let it go, and take upon oneself the form of a bondservant, one who is sold out completely to Christ.

Mary, the mother of Jesus, was such a bondservant. She said, "Behold, the bondslave [or handmaiden] of the Lord" (Luke 1:38). Mary gave up the right to herself.

As daughters of the most high God, women must give up their rights and esteem their husbands as better than themselves. (See Philippians 2:3.)

An excellent passage for wives who have marital problems, whether they have believing husbands or not, is 1 Peter 3:1–6. Let's look at each verse, using the Amplified Bible, for those Christlike attitudes a woman needs.

1 Peter 3:1: "In like manner you married women, be submissive to your own husbands— subordinate yourselves as being secondary to and dependent on them, and adapt yourselves to them. So that even if they do not obey the Word [of God], they may be won over not by discussion but by the [godly] lives of their wives."

It is not easy to subordinate yourself, but it is worth it. In so doing, you will have a good marriage, you will be changed, and you will grow into a mature Christian—one who glorifies God with her life.

As we grow, we will develop the heart attitudes found in 1 Peter 3:1. They are as follows:

Submissiveness. The act of yielding in obedience.

Subordination. Coming under the authority of a superior.

Jesus always went back to the Father. He did nothing of Himself. In the marriage relationship the wife must learn to go back to her authority; she does not move outside the God-given authority of her husband.

Dependence. Depending on another for aid and support.

Many men do not become the men God wants them to be because their wives are independent. These wives do not encourage the development of godly traits in their husbands because they are ready and eager to have control. They do not let their husbands know that they need their help and assistance, which would help those husbands to take on their godly responsibilities.

Adaptability. Ability to make suitable adjustments to someone else's requirements.

A wife adapts herself to her husband. She fits into his plans. Many a woman is so independent that she functions almost as though she did not have a husband. She thinks without considering the needs of her husband, so that she is in the center and God is on the sideline.

Her relationship with God is wrong. She needs to ask God to show her the ways she has failed to have a right relationship with Him, and ask Him to forgive her.

We are such self-centered creatures that we take control away from God almost unknowingly. Our minds must be renewed so that we will constantly put Him in the center.

As a husband observes the qualities that are being built into his wife, as she submits to God and desires to be like Christ, he will change. He will see it, not merely hear it.

What will he see?

1 Peter 3:2: "The pure and modest way in which you conduct yourselves, together with your reverence [for your husband. That is, you are to feel for him all that reverence includes]—to respect, defer to, revere him; [revere means] to honor, esteem (appreciate, prize), and [in the human sense] adore him; [and adore means] to admire, praise, be devoted to, deeply love and enjoy [your husband]."

He will see the following attitudes or qualities in his wife:

Purity and Modesty. In thought, word, deed, and dress, demonstrating Christ's presence.

A woman should dress so that what she wears draws attention to her face, not to her body. That includes wearing colors that compliment her face. Everything, even color, is important to God, who after all created a wonderfully colorful world.

Respect. Many women do not respect their husbands because they have difficulty finding anything to respect. They have been so busy looking at the sin in their husbands' lives that they have been unable to see the qualities God has placed in these men.

This violates Matthew 7:5, which tells us to take the log out of our own eye before we try to take the speck out of someone else's eye. As the wife deals with the sin in her own heart, suddenly she will see her husband in a new light and gain new respect for him.

Giving Honor and Esteem. The Bible teaches us to esteem one another as better than ourselves. (See Philippians 2:3–4.) In marriage the wife is to esteem her husband as better than herself.

Giving Admiration and Praise. God created a man with an ego. That ego causes him to want to go out and earn money for his family and to protect his family.

His ego needs to be built up by his wife. There are women—some of them unscrupulous, and even some who are Christians—who will admire and praise him if the wife does not. They care little that he is married.

So it is up to the wife to admire and praise her husband, to be eager to give honest compliments, and to show that she cares about how he looks by the care she gives to his clothes, his home, his children.

Showing Devotion. Devotion means to be loyal and true. One who is devoted never takes part in conversations that criticize or destroy, and does not spend time building up a backlog of criticism.

Showing Deep Love and Enjoyment. A wife who deeply loves and enjoys her husband can listen to him tell the same stories over and over again.

She loves to see him. She love to hear his voice. She loves to watch him teach or preach or water the garden or whatever he does. It builds her up, causes her to love him more, and it will change their marriage.

In the next three verses Peter gives four more attitudes a wife needs to develop:

1 Peter 3:3–5: "Let not yours be the [merely] external adorning with [elaborate] interweaving and knotting of the hair, the wearing of jewelry, or changes of clothes; but let it be the inward adorning and beauty of the hidden person of the heart, with the incorruptible and unfading charm of a gentle and peaceful spirit, which (is not anxious or wrought up, but) is very precious in the sight of God. For it was thus that the pious women of old who hoped in God were (accustomed) to beautify themselves, and were submissive to their husbands—adapting themselves to them as themselves secondary and dependent upon them."

Inner Beauty. Wives should concentrate on the inner beauty—the unfading charm—and not merely on the outward adorning. Inner beauty is produced by a woman's relationship with the Lord Jesus, and it never fades.

Some of the most beautiful women are those who have known and walked with God for many years and have a deep relationship with Him.

Gentleness, Peacefulness, Lack of Anxiousness. These qualities, especially not being anxious, are very important in a relationship. Peter says that Sarah exemplified this lack of anxiety; and he uses her example to point out more heart attitudes for the wife to develop.

1 Peter 3:6: "It was thus that Sarah obeyed Abraham (following his guidance and acknowledging his headship over her by) calling him lord—master, leader, authority. And you are now her true daughters if you do right and let nothing terrify you—not giving way to hysterical fears or letting anxieties unnerve you."

Twice Sarah had to enter the harem of an unrighteous king. In this, she was submitting to her husband, but most of all she was trusting in God. Because of that, God did not remember Sarah's shortcomings; He remembered that she respected and understood authority, and called Abraham *lord.*

God is saying to us that a woman is to have the same attitude toward her husband that Sarah had toward Abraham, trusting God to work through him. This leads us to the next characteristic of the godly wife:

Following Her Husband's Guidance. God gives direction to the husband first regarding major moves and decisions. He then gives a confirming word to the wife. Guidance comes to the man as head, not to the woman. (See Ephesians 5:23–24.)

Acknowledging His Headship, Calling Him Lord, Not Panicking! The development of these heart attitudes will produce a very special kind of spirit:

Reverent Spirit. She becomes a woman who fears the Lord. (See Proverbs 31:30.)

Servant's Spirit. Jesus set the example. (See Philippians 2:3–8.)

Grateful Spirit. Her hope rests in God. (See Psalm 62:5.)

Quiet Spirit. This pleases God. (See 1 Peter 3:4.)

A woman who has submitted her heart to God and developed these attributes receives praise from different sources:

Her children rise up and bless her.

Her husband also praises her, saying, "Many daughters have done nobly, but you excel them all."

Her works praise her.

A woman who fears the Lord shall be praised. (See Proverbs 31:28–31.)

22.4 A WOMAN'S FULFILLMENT

A woman finds fulfillment, identity, and purpose in life as she carries out her God-given responsibilities.

God intends for the home to be the center of a mother's world. When she chooses an outside vocation, she weakens her marriage, lessens the influence she has on her children, exposes herself to dangerous temptations, and violates God's principles for a wife and mother.

Choosing an outside vocation also forces her to

choose between two worlds. It violates the Scripture, "No one can serve two masters" (Matthew 6:24). She runs the risk of becoming a divided, doubleminded person.

But she becomes singleminded when she focuses on her husband, her children, and her home. She gains strength through that singular focus.

God's "good and acceptable and perfect" plan for women (see Romans 12:2) involves that they carry out several important functions.

Be Workers at Home. Paul encourages young wives "to be sensible, pure, workers at home, kind, being subject to their own husbands, that the word of God may not be dishonored" (Titus 2:5).

Has it ever occurred to some mothers that working outside the home and pursuing a career might dishonor God's Word? Single women who have no choice, and married women without children are in a different situation. But a woman with children needs to be at home so that God's Word is not dishonored.

Train and Teach the Children. "And you shall teach [the Word of God] diligently to your sons and shall talk of them when you sit in your house and when you walk by the way and when you lie down and when you rise up" (Deuteronomy 6:7).

The teaching of children is carried on every moment of every day, not just at certain times, and even when children are older. Mothers need to be at home in the morning when their children go to school and in the afternoon when they come home. Those can count among the most precious moments a mother has with her children. She should make that a priority, so that her children can talk with her and the communication lines remain open.

Be Resourcefully Productive. Proverbs 31 describes a woman who has built a good home:

"She looks for wool and flax, And works with her hands in delight. She senses that her gain is good; Her lamp does not go out at night. She is not afraid of the snow for her household, For all her household are clothed with scarlet. She makes coverings for herself; Her clothing is fine linen and purple. She looks well to the ways of her household, And does not eat the bread of idleness" (verses 13, 18, 21–22, 27).

A wife has no time to sit in front of the television for several hours a day. That and other pursuits distract a woman from finishing what is necessary in order to relieve the burden of her responsibilities. Then when her husband comes home, she is free to tend to his needs without unfinished work hanging over her head.

Teach Younger Women. "Older women likewise are to be reverent in their behavior . . . teaching what is good, that they may encourage the young women to love their husbands" (Titus 2:3–4).

A woman can have great joy in teaching younger women the principles about marriage that God has taught her. She can do this in a Bible study or prayer group or in a one-to-one friendship, wherever God provides the opportunity.

Show Hospitality. Romans 12:13 includes "practicing hospitality" as a mark of Christian behavior. "To divide your bread with the hungry, And bring the homeless poor into the house" (Isaiah 58:7) is a worthy aim for a godly woman.

Jesus said, "I was hungry, and you gave Me something to eat; I was thirsty, and you gave Me drink; I was a stranger, and you invited Me in" (Matthew 25:35).

22.5 QUALITIES OF A WIFE

The Bible contains qualities of an ungodly wife and a godly wife. Proverbs 5:3–6 and 7:11, 19 define an ungodly woman as one who has smooth speech and is bitter, unstable, unthinking, boisterous, rebellious, and unfaithful to her husband.

Isaiah 3:12 indicates that because of sin women rule over men: "O My people! Their oppressors are children, and women rule over them. O My people! Those who guide you lead you astray, and confuse the direction of your paths."

Isaiah 32:9–10 warns that women who are complacent and at ease will surely be troubled: "Rise up you women who are at ease, And hear my voice; Give ear to my word, You complacent daughters. Within a year and a few days, You will be troubled, O complacent daughters."

Paul cautions that in the last days difficult times will come. Men will enter households and "captivate weak women weighed down with sins, led on by various impulses, always learning and never able to come to the knowledge of the truth" (2 Timothy 3:6–7).

And Paul instructs younger widows to marry; otherwise they will learn to be idle "gossips and busybodies, talking about things not proper to mention" (1 Timothy 5:13).

The passage in Proverbs 31, on the other hand, lists the many desirable qualities of a godly wife.

An excellent wife is worth far more than jewels (verse 10).

The heart of her husband trusts in her, and he will never lack benefits (verse 11).

She does him good all her life (verse 12).

She provides for the needs of her household (verses 14–15, 27).

She works hard, for long hours, and is strong (verses 14–15, 17–19).

She has wisdom, dignity, and peace, and is pleasant and kind (verses 16, 25–26).

She cares for others (verses 15, 20–21).

Her husband is known and respected (verse 23).

Her husband and children praise her (verse 28).

She fears the Lord (verse 30).

22.6 A HUSBAND'S BASIC NEEDS

Every man has different needs. A wife will want to find out what particular needs her husband has. Listed below are seven basic needs husbands share in common.

A husband needs a wife who respects him as a man.

A husband needs a wife who accepts him as leader and believes in his God-given responsibilities.

A husband needs a wife who will continue to develop inward and outward beauty.

A husband needs a wife who can lovingly appeal to him when he is going beyond his limitations, and can respond wisely to those who question his ideas, goals, or motives.

A husband needs quality time to be alone with himself and with God.

A husband needs a wife who is grateful for all he has done and is doing for her.

A husband needs a wife who will be praised by other people for her character and her good works.

22.7 TEN COMMANDMENTS FOR WIVES

These "ten commandments" provide important guidelines for wives to follow in order to be the women God has called them to be.

1. Honor your own womanhood, that your day may be long in the house that your husband has provided for you.

A wife should honor the fact that she is a woman and set her mind on (in other words, obey) those things God has told her to do. (See Proverbs 31.)

2. Do not expect your husband to give you as many luxuries as your father has given you after many years of hard work.

Wives are to be content no matter what the circumstances, and with whatever their husbands provide. (See Philippians 4:11 and 1 Timothy 6:6.) When wives become content, God can change the circumstances or teach them to overcome the difficulties. Meanwhile, they can ask God to multiply and use creatively what they have.

3. Do not forget the virtues of good humor, for all that a man has he will give for a woman's smile.

Proverbs 17:22 says that "a merry heart doeth good like a medicine" (KJV). A husband who comes home carrying the burdens of the day needs to laugh and have fun with his wife. Laughter lifts a heavy spirit.

4. Do not nag.

Solomon wrote, "It is better to live in a desert land than with a contentious and vexing woman" (Proverbs 21:19). Also, "It is better to live in a corner of the roof than in a house shared with a contentious woman" (Proverbs 25:24).

Because women are detail-oriented, they talk about details. That can turn into nagging. If a woman has a need or problem, she takes it to God first and then appeals to her husband. But she does not nag. (See Proverbs 10:19.)

5. You shall coddle your husband, for every man loves to be fussed over.

Doing what pleases him, such as making his favorite dinner or dessert, can perk up a wilting marriage.

6. Remember that the frank approval of your husband is worth far more to you than the sidelong glances of many strangers.

A wife is to please God first, then please her husband, and let God take care of everybody else.

7. Do not forget the grace of cleanliness and good dressing.

This keeps the spirit of the marriage alive. A woman who becomes slothful and negligent of her appearance says she does not care about herself or what her husband thinks of her.

How a husband sees his wife in the morning when he leaves for work is how he remembers her throughout the day. It takes only a few moments to freshen up. She should also spend time letting him know she will miss him.

8. Permit no one to assure you that you are having a hard time of it—neither your mother, nor your sister, nor your maiden aunt, nor any of your kinfolk—for the Judge will not hold her guiltless who lets another discredit her husband.

If a woman is having a problem with her

husband, she should not tell her family about it. If she needs counseling, she should seek a counselor. (See Psalm 39:1 and Proverbs 13:3.)

Above all, she must not talk about her husband with other women, especially not in a Bible study. Women do a great disservice to their husbands and displease God when they talk about them.

9. Keep your home with all diligence, for out of it come the joys of your old age.

A wife who fails to take care of her husband, her family, and her home *now* will discover she has no relationship with her husband when the children leave home. She will have no desire to stay in that home.

Her vision is wrong. Many marriages of thirty years end in divorce because no vision exists for the home and the marriage relationship. Scripture says that "where there is no vision, the people perish" (Proverbs 29:18). We need to have a vision and an understanding of the importance of the home and marriage; and we need to nurture that marital relationship.

Marriage can be compared to a plant. A plant needs to be watered, to have sun, to be turned so it can receive the sun evenly, and to be weeded and cultivated, in order to grow. In the same way, marriage requires care and work; it doesn't just happen.

10. Commit your ways unto the Lord your God, and your children will rise up and call you blessed (see Proverbs 31:28).

All of a mother's times of being alone; all the sacrifices; all the nights of staying up when the children were sick or to be sure they were safe at home in bed; all the concerts, ballgames, school programs, and PTA meetings—all are worth it when her child rises up and calls her blessed.

A woman must ask herself, "Is my desire to satisfy myself, or is my desire to please God?" God is pleased by a godly wife and mother who dies to herself and gives herself first to God, then to her husband, then to her children, and finally to the Body of Christ.

Doing this will produce fruit in a woman's life and peace in her heart. She will be a blessing to God, her husband, her children, and other believers. And the Word of God will be honored.

Chapter 23

THE HUSBAND'S ROLE

God created a husband to surrender his life to Jesus Christ so that his family will find Christ by his example. And God designed him to be the head of his wife. (See Ephesians 5:23–24.) A husband must be willing to lay down his life in loving service to his wife so that she willingly gives her submission to him.

A husband provides for his family a mantle of protection whose substance is his belonging to and trusting in God. As he is rooted and grounded in God's love, and as he obeys God, he is like the man who built his house upon a rock, enabling his wife and children to dwell restfully within that house. (See Matthew 7:26.)

A godly peace will settle upon the home of a family that fits into God's plan for them. It makes a difference. When wives give their lives to Jesus Christ and to their husbands, and when husbands give their lives to Jesus Christ and to their wives, they reap a rich and overflowing blessing.

23.1 ATTITUDES OF A GODLY HUSBAND

How does a husband acquire godly attitudes? It starts with a decision: He must want to be a godly husband, purposing in his heart to achieve that goal. He must be honest with God in evaluating himself as a husband. To avoid falling into ungodly thought patterns and attitudes, he must trust and obey God. Then, the more he gives of himself to God and his wife, the more God will bless him.

If he gives nothing, he will receive nothing: that is the principle of sowing and reaping. (See Galatians 6:7–9.)

A man pictures what he wants in his marriage as a godly husband. It is far more than having sex and a housekeeper which, unfortunately, is the impression many husbands have given their wives. Wives are not just bedpartners or maids or slaves to do their husbands' bidding. That is not a Christlike relationship. The husband must see the big picture of the marriage and of the one God has given to him by covenant. That is the beginning.

The way of humility, brokenness, and blessings is the step-by-step path to becoming a godly husband. Rarely does a habit change overnight. Rather, God builds new behavior patterns into both spouses over a period of time. Out of a husband's humility and brokenness, God blesses the home.

A godly husband refuses to slip back into the past. He does not rest on his accomplishments or wallow in his failures. He moves ahead to the new things God has for him.

He is conscious of his wealth in Christ and in the wife He has given him. God-consciousness must always precede wife-consciousness. This will lead him to love, honor, and cherish her. Men who are insensitive to God will be insensitive to their wives. Problems with God will develop into problems with the wife.

A husband has a great responsibility. If he is to love his wife as Christ loves the church, he must give of himself to his wife. A husband who loves and cherishes his wife builds self-esteem and fulfillment into her.

23.2 ATTRIBUTES OF A GODLY HUSBAND

A man has two sides; strength and sensitivity. Often a man shows his strength without showing his sensitivity. This is part of the logical makeup of a man. Men are generally bold, even dogmatic, in their logic, while women are more detailed and emotional. Together they balance and complement one another. Out of that balance men need to understand and be sensitive to their wives.

Strength. A woman wants to see her husband as a leader, a protector, and a provider. God created woman with a hunger for someone in whom to feel secure. She needs above all to feel secure in the Lord, of course, but He has given her a head of her household. She needs to feel that comfort and peace in her husband as he fulfills his God-given responsibility. A husband who does not do that fails his wife and God.

A woman also wants to see her husband as a contributor to society, not in the world's ways, but in the life of Christ spilling over and touching and changing society.

A woman wants her husband to be masculine. She wants him to have good character. She feels comfortable when he is confident in his daily walk with God, in his marriage, and in his family. A woman wants her husband to be strong and in good health.

Sensitivity. A godly husband attempts to understand his wife. He is sensitive to her and does not ridicule or belittle her if she responds to something in an emotional way. With her he is always gentle, attending to her, aware of her presence and the nice things she does, of the way she dresses, of the meals she prepares. He *sees* his wife and what she does.

A godly husband is youthful, even as he grows older. He feels good spiritually, physically, mentally, emotionally.

He is humble, demonstrating a servant's heart to his wife.

And he is refined. Refinement is expressed in dress, cleanliness, good manners and speech.

A strong man makes women and children feel secure; he stirs up the admiration of all and makes a woman feel womanly. A sensitive man promotes good human relations among all people; he awakens love and respect in women and children.

A godly man rules his home in firmness, kindness, and love. He can say no firmly to his wife, and make her feel secure by doing so. They may talk over a matter, but the final decision rests with him. If he says no, she appreciates his firmness. Right or wrong, he has made a decision, and she feels comfortable, knowing God will honor it.

A man makes his most notable contribution to his family, the world, and the Kingdom of God when he functions well as the leader, protector, and provider; when he rules his home with firmness, kindness, and love, with the necessary security and comforts; and when his children develop into happy, well-adjusted citizens.

God has placed the man as head of his home. As such, the characteristics for an overseer or bishop of the church, as listed in 1 Timothy 3:2–4, also apply to a husband. God has ordained him to be:

- An overseer—head of his household.
- Above reproach—of good reputation; strengthening his spirit and not his flesh.
- A husband of one wife—committed to the permanency of marriage.
- Temperate—self-controlled.
- Prudent—sensible.
- Respectable—worthy of respect; respected in his community and family.
- Hospitable—generous.
- Able to teach—setting an example by word and deed.
- Not addicted to alcohol—free from bondage to habits that are not pleasing to God.
- Peaceable—a peacemaker.
- Gentle—considerate, sensitive to his wife and children.
- Uncontentious—not involved in competitive striving.
- Free from the love of money—not in bondage to money.
- Manages his household well—carrying out his role as head.
- Disciplines his children well—trains and corrects them. (Primarily his responsibility to see it is done, although his wife enters in.)

The husband who fulfills these characteristics has consideration for his wife and honors her as the weaker vessel. Anything less than honoring her and living with her in an understanding way will hinder a husband's prayers. (See 1 Peter 3:7.) God holds him accountable.

23.3 GODLY GOALS

The Bible gives us qualities of a godly husband. Some are noted below, alongside the qualities of an ungodly husband.

Godly	Ungodly
Head of the wife (Ephesians 5:23)	Refuses responsibilities
Loves his wife as Christ loves the church (Ephesians 5:25)	Demands only that his senses be gratified
Nourishes and cherishes his wife (Ephesians 5:28–29)	Rejects her
Rejoices in the wife of his youth (Proverbs 5:18)	Adulterous relationships
Trusts his wife (Proverbs 31:11)	Distrusts his wife
Praises his wife (Proverbs 31:28b–29)	Slanders his wife
Is not harsh with his wife (Colossians 3:19)	Abuses his wife
Lives in an understanding way with his wife (1 Peter 3:7)	Concerned only with self
Honors his wife (1 Peter 3:7)	Dishonors her
Does not rule over his own body (1 Corinthians 7:3–4)	Refuses sexual rights
Pleases his wife (1 Corinthians 7:33)	Ignores his wife
Answers his wife's questions (1 Corinthians 14:35)	Fails to communicate
Provides for his family (1 Timothy 5:8)	Neglects family

HANDBOOK FOR HELPING OTHERS

23.4 A WIFE'S BASIC NEEDS

A man can better understand his wife if he knows what her basic needs are.

She needs the stability and direction of a spiritual leader.

She needs to know she is meeting vital needs in her husband's life and work that no other woman can meet.

She needs to see and hear that her husband cherishes her and delights in her as a person.

She needs to know that her husband understands her by protecting her in areas of her limitation.

She needs to know that her husband enjoys setting aside quality time for intimate conversation with her.

She needs to know that her husband is aware of her presence even when his mind is on other matters.

She needs to see that her husband is making investments in her life that will expand and fulfill her world.

23.5 TEN COMMANDMENTS FOR HUSBANDS

Husbands will want to consider and apply these "ten commandments" in their families.

1. Remember that your wife is your partner by covenant, and not your property.

2. Do not expect your wife to be your wife and wage-earner at the same time.

God is our source, our provider. He is not affected by the world's economy. When a man thinks his wife has to go to work to help support the family, he is saying God is not big enough to provide for their needs. Then when she is unable to fulfill her role at home and the family life disintegrates, a man may blame God for the problems.

There are indeed times and situations when a woman may work outside the house, but these instances must be God-prompted, not because of the need for some material possession.

3. Do not think your business is none of your wife's business.

Some areas may not require dialogue, but for the most part, husbands need desperately to communicate with their wives. If a husband is hurting, he should tell his wife. Then she can support him with her prayers and encouragement.

4. You shall hold your wife's love by the same means you won it.

The honeymoon is never over. Keep it exciting. One hug and kiss in the morning may carry the husband through the day. But at least a second hug and kiss will delight his wife, make her feel more secure, and build up her self-esteem.

5. You shall make the building of your home your first business.

Husbands are to be home-builders, not home-destroyers.

6. You shall cooperate with your wife in establishing family discipline.

Too many parents disagree on how to discipline, and even argue over it in front of the children. It is better to go to another room and settle the disagreement, and then discipline the child. In the end, the husband decides. The wife may appeal his decision, but she must yield to him. He is accountable before God for his decision, right or wrong.

7. You shall enter your house with cheerfulness.

The husband comes home from work after a particularly trying day. His wife has been waiting for him to come home so she can pour her life into his. Instead of "dumping" his burdens on his wife the moment he walks in the door, he greets her cheerfully and positively. Then he tells her about the trials of the day, and she is better able to listen and support him.

Timing is important. He is not to unload all the cares of the world at the doorstep. And she is there to build him up and also to be built up by him.

8. You shall not let anyone criticize your wife to your face and get away with it—neither your father, nor your mother, nor your brothers, nor your relatives.

It is simply not God's intent that a husband belittle his wife, or that he allow anyone else to belittle her without taking a stand against it. The husband and wife have a covenant relationship, and both need to support one another, individually and together, in whatever circumstances, against all criticism.

Even if his wife makes a mistake, the husband is not to correct her in front of others. He goes to her privately and in love.

9. You shall not take your wife for granted.

Husbands expect their wives to be there when they come home, with dinner ready and their clothes clean. Never forget to say, "Honey, that was a great meal," or, "I really appreciate the way you keep my clothes clean and neat."

10. Remember your home, to keep it holy.

23.6 A HUSBAND'S OFFERING TO HIS WIFE

Without Christ a husband has little to offer his wife. But with Christ he offers her:

Praise. "Her children rise up and bless her; Her husband also, and he praises her" (Proverbs 31:28).

Inspiration. "Many daughters have done nobly, But you excel them all" (Proverbs 31:29).

Understanding. Love "bears all things, believes all things, hopes all things, endures all things" (1 Corinthians 13:7).

Trust. "The heart of her husband trusts in her, And he will have no lack of gain" (Proverbs 31:11).

Consideration. "Likewise you husbands, live considerately with your wives, bestowing honor on the woman as the weaker sex, since you are joint heirs of the grace of life, in order that your prayers may not be hindered" (1 Peter 3:7, RSV).

Service. "Do nothing from selfishness or empty conceit, but with humility of mind let each of you regard one another as more important than himself; do not merely look out for your own personal interests, but also for the interests of others [your wife]" (Philippians 2:3–4).

Forgiveness. "And be kind to one another, tender-hearted, forgiving each other, just as God in Christ also has forgiven you" (Ephesians 4:32).

Encouragement. "Therefore encourage one another and build up one another, just as you also are doing" (1 Thessalonians 5:11).

23.7 CONSIDERATIONS

Husbands and fathers need to consider these questions regarding their families.

Is your relationship with your wife built on tolerance or acceptance?

Some husbands simply tolerate their wives, but the Bible says, "Wherefore, accept one another, just as Christ also accepted us to the glory of God" (Romans 15:7).

Do you see your wife as a competitor or as a companion?

Again, the Bible provides an answer: "The Lord has been a witness between you and the wife of your youth, against whom you have dealt treacherously, though she is your companion and your wife by covenant" (Malachi 2:14).

Is your wife a widow and are your children orphans?

Many men "do their own thing." They go off to the golf course or local fishing hole without consulting their wives or children. They just tell them. But that is not living considerately. That is not love.

Men who do this in a sense make their wives widows and their children orphans. Their wives need a husband; their children need a father. "Therefore whatever you want others to do for you, do so for them" (Matthew 7:12).

23.8 MARITAL CONFLICTS

Conflicts in marriage are good and natural. The very nature of the relationship—male and female, logic and emotion—produces conflicts.

But balance can be achieved in a relationship based on a covenant agreement. Resolved conflicts can be healthy in producing that balance. Unresolved conflicts lead to a sinful response.

The eight major conflicts in marriage center on religion, sex, finances, in-laws, recreation, communication, children, and work. The intensity of conflict depends on how quickly each partner allows the Holy Spirit to lead him or her to settle it. God wants the husband to respond biblically to each conflict.

Religion. A man led by the Spirit will direct his family to the church God chooses. He will provide the spiritual leadership in his home through prayer and reading God's Word, thereby setting a godly example for his family to follow.

The husband's responsibility is the spiritual leadership of the home. It is not the wife's responsibility to set the spiritual atmosphere. She is part of the peace and quietness that fills the home, while God holds husbands accountable for the spiritual climate in the household. "For I have chosen him, in order that he may command his children and his household after him to keep the way of the Lord" (Genesis 18:19).

Sex. How does God view sex between a husband and wife?

A husband participates in the sexual relationship as his wife's lover. A lover is one who cherishes the life of the other. True marital happiness is found when a husband is willing to lay down his life and desires to bring joy and fulfillment to his wife. A wife must be assured of her husband's love for her, so that she can willingly respond to him.

A man looks at the sexual relationship differently from the way a woman looks at it. A woman sees it as a very deep expression of love. A man tends to see it as a means of physical release. If a man sees it only as that, however, conflict arises, because the wife feels used and abused—an object. The husband needs to redirect his focus, letting his involvement become an act of love. The wife then receives it as such and responds accordingly, and it is beautiful.

Sex between a husband and wife is a spiritual experience because God ordained it. We need to see every part of our body—the creative processes and our sexual involvement—through spiritual eyes. If we do, sex will be holy, good, and pure. Sex is to be participated in as unto God. Then it becomes fulfilling for both husband and wife. (See Genesis 2:24; 1 Corinthians 7:3a; Ephesians 5:31.)

Finances. In obedience to God's Word, a man gives to God, pays taxes to the government, and provides for the financial well-being of his family.

As head of the household, the husband is responsible for preparing the budget and paying the bills in agreement with his wife. His wife depends on him so that she and the children might live peacefully in the home he provides.

"But if any one does not provide for his own, and especially for those of his household, he has denied the faith, and is worse than an unbeliever" (1 Timothy 5:8).

Some wives take care of the finances because they want the control; others because their husbands refuse to do it. But God's heart is for the husband to be responsible for the finances in the home, if he is physically able.

The major way for a wife to depend on her husband is to let him manage the finances; otherwise, she will be independent. God never intended the wife to carry the burden of the family's finances, except in special situations. He spoke to Adam first, in matters of guidance to Joseph and to other biblical men. He ordained that man function in headship.

The husband should consult his wife on major purchases. But she is not to worry about whether the electric bill and other bills are paid. God in her husband will take care of those bills, which frees her to be the homemaker God ordained her to be.

What can a wife do if her husband forces her to manage the finances? She can appeal to him honestly and to God, then trust God to make the changes. (See Matthew 22:21.)

In-Laws. In-laws must not control the marriage. Each new family unit needs to separate itself from the old families and cleave to one another. A man should free himself from any bondage to his parents, his relatives, and his friends. Disobedience to God's Word concerning the marriage relationship leads to problems with in-laws.

Leisure Time (Recreation). A man should consider and consult with his wife and family as to their needs and desires for recreation. At times he may need to go hunting, fishing, or the like, and his wife should let him go. But it should be by agreement. Family outings should also be by mutual consent.

Communication. It is vitally important for husbands and wives to talk. A man who has difficulty communicating with his wife and family is probably having difficulty communicating with God. He must communicate with his family in order to produce a climate of mutual love, acceptance, and understanding that results in family harmony and fulfillment.

The following are guidelines accompanied by Scriptures which, if followed, will help husbands and wives communicate more effectively. In any situation, a husband should be slow to speak, and ask himself the following:

1. Do I really have the facts?
"He who gives an answer before he hears, it is folly and shame to him" (Proverbs 18:13).

2. Is what I would like to say profitable? Will it help or hurt? Be constructive or destructive?
"Let no unwholesome word proceed from your mouth, but only such a word as is good for edification according to the need of the moment, that it may give grace to those who hear" (Ephesians 4:29; see also Proverbs 20:15 and Romans 15:1-2).

3. Is this the proper time for me to say it, or would it be better for me to wait?
"A man has joy in an apt answer, And how delightful is a timely word" (Proverbs 15:23; see also Proverbs 15:28 and 25:11-12).

4. Is my attitude right?
"And be kind to one another, tender-hearted, forgiving each other, just as God in Christ also has

forgiven you" (Ephesians 4:32; see also 1 Corinthians 16:14 and Ephesians 4:15).

5. Are the words I will use the best possible way of saying it?

"A gentle answer turns away wrath, But a harsh word stirs up anger" (Proverbs 15:1; see also Proverbs 12:25; 16:23; Ecclesiastes 12:10).

6. Have I prayed about this matter, and am I trusting God to help me?

"Trust in the Lord with all your heart, And do not lean on your own understanding. In all your ways acknowledge Him, and He will make your paths straight" (Proverbs 3:5–6; see also Psalm 19:14 and Colossians 4:2–6).

Children.   A man must always set a godly example for his children to follow. This includes using God's Word for teaching, reproof, correction, and training. The father should spend quality time with each child, showing love, understanding and encouragement.

He should not exasperate his children, "that they may not lose heart" (Colossians 3:21).

"And these words, which I am commanding you today, shall be on your heart; and you shall teach them diligently to your sons and shall talk of them when you sit in your house and when you walk by the way and when you lie down and when you rise up" (Deuteronomy 6:6–7; see also 1 Samuel 3:12–14.)

Work.   A man's work should provide for the material needs of his household while allowing time to meet the personal and spiritual needs of his family.

". . . to make it your ambition to lead a quiet life

and attend to your own business and work with your hands, just as we commanded you; so that you may behave properly toward outsiders and not be in any need" (1 Thessalonians 4:11–12; see also Ephesians 4:28 and 1 Timothy 5:8.)

23.9 CONFLICT RESOLUTION

Conflict resolution involves several important steps.

A husband and wife need to be honest about themselves, willing to admit they may be at fault. They need humility to listen and ask for forgiveness.

They should never try to hurt or get even with the other. Respect, admiration, and trust must abide in a marriage. If either partner wants to hurt the other, that one should stop awhile; remove himself or herself from a confrontation, if necessary; take time to collect his or her thoughts; and regain a right perspective. Prayer is the best action, letting God restore self-control.

A husband or wife should always say those three important words, "I forgive you." To say an offense is "okay" is both a lie and an insult. Until the Lord Jesus cleanses a person, there is no "okay-ness," no matter what we think or feel.

A husband and wife must settle their conflicts to prevent sinful responses from developing. Conflicts can become opportunities for bringing balance into the home.

Both husband and wife have good qualities and bad. They talk about the good and let God deal with the bad. They encourage one another in their growth to spiritual maturity.

As unto the bow the cord is,

So unto man is woman.
Though she bends him,
She obeys him,
Though she draws him,
Yet she follows,
Useless each without the other.

Hiawatha
Henry W. Longfellow

What good is a husband without a wife or a wife without a husband?

Chapter 24

BUILDING A GODLY HOME

Whether a man and woman are entering marriage for the first time, or have experienced the trauma of divorce or the death of a spouse, there are goals and responsibilities they will want to fulfill. How does a couple build a godly home?

24.1 SUBMISSION

Christians talk about the important of submission in marriage, but not always with a clear understanding of what it means and what the Bible teaches.

Wives who try to submit to their husbands and fail are trying to do it on their own through good deeds. Submission is an attitude of the heart for all of us, men and women alike. But in the marriage relationship God calls the woman to have a submissive attitude for a specific purpose.

"And be subject to one another in the fear of Christ" (Ephesians 5:21). Some wives use this verse as an excuse for not submitting to their husbands. Indeed, mutual subjection *is* a goal for both partners, but they can achieve it only by following God's plan.

In Ephesians 5:22–33, an excellent passage for studying marriage roles and responsibilities, God speaks to the wife first. She is the key to a happy marriage. She can, as we have already seen, either make or break a home. She needs to understand her role and obey God's call for her life, leaning on Him for His love and support.

"Wives, be subject to your own husbands, as to the Lord. For the husband is the head of the wife, as Christ also is the head of the church, He Himself being the Savior of the body. But as the church is subject to Christ, so also the wives ought to be to their husbands in everything" (Ephesians 5:22–24).

If wives are having a problem submitting to their husbands, they are also having a problem submitting to God. A woman pleases God by submitting to her husband. But the woman who by choice or circumstances has her husband in submission to her disobeys God's Word.

Even if, as many wives say, their husbands do not assume their position as head of the house, wives are not therefore to take over. How long is a woman willing to wait for her husband to come to that place of leadership? Thirty minutes? Thirty years? God's way is for wives to be subject to their husbands. Taking that first step of submission and committing it to God will change husbands.

24.2 LOVE

While the wife is the key to a happy home, the man has the weightier responsibility:

"Husbands, love your wives, just as Christ also loved the church and gave Himself up for her; that He might sanctify her, having cleansed her by the washing of water with the word, that He might present to Himself the church in all her glory, having no spot or wrinkle or any such thing; but that she should be holy and blameless. So husbands ought also to love their own wives as their own bodies. He who loves his own wife loves himself; for no one ever hated his own flesh, but nourishes and cherishes it, just as Christ also does the church, because we are members of His body" (Ephesians 5:25–30).

Are husbands willing to lay down their lives for their wives? Jesus loved us that much, even with our spots and blemishes. Husbands are to love their wives—and wives their husbands—in the same way, with their spots and blemishes.

The second step to a happy home, then, is a husband who obeys God and loves his wife as Christ loves the church. It takes time for a man to learn to love his wife with God's love. Could a woman take being loved the way Christ loves His bride, the Church? Would it not transform her, as it would transform any of us to experience fully the depth of God's love? Husbands are to pour on that love in abundance.

The more wives submit to their husbands, and the more husbands love their wives, the more they fulfill God's purpose for them.

"For this cause a man shall leave his father and mother, and shall cleave to his wife; and the two shall become one flesh. This mystery is great; but I am speaking with reference to Christ and the church. Nevertheless let each individual among you also love his own wife even as himself; and let the wife see to it that she respect her husband" (Ephesians 5:31–33).

24.3 ONE FLESH

The third step to a godly home finds a wife and her husband becoming one flesh.

Until a husband and wife practice the roles God has assigned to each, they cannot be in mutual subjection to one another as Ephesians 5:21 instructs.

As a man and wife draw closer to God, they become closer in their relationship with each other. The farther they get from God, on the other hand, the farther they grow from each other.

A marriage has a far greater likelihood of lasting when a couple fits into God's design for their lives. Rebellion against God will block the movement of the Holy Spirit between God and man, resulting in an unproductive relationship and unanswered prayers. (See Psalm 66:18 and 1 Peter 3:7). Obedience to God's Word, as well as a Christlike attitude, will produce a godly, fruitful marriage.

(Other Scriptures to study on marriage roles and responsibilities are Genesis 3:16; Proverbs 5:18; 12:4; 14:1; 1 Corinthians 11:3, 7–9; Colossians 3:18–19; 2 Timothy 3:6–7; Hebrews 13:4; 1 Peter 2:18–25; 3:1–7.)

24.4 LOOKING TO GOD

A problem can arise when a wife thinks she has an unspiritual husband, whether he is a believer or not. Even though he may be consciously acting against God's will, she is to respect him. (See Ephesians 5:33.) She sets her mind on spiritual things by looking to God, not at her husband or circumstances, and thanking God for him, not demanding change.

In the order that results, God's blessings will come. Satan cannot touch our families if husbands and wives assume their God-ordained roles. The choice is ours. Either we choose God's way and bring God's peace, joy and blessings of obedience into our homes, or we choose our own way and destroy our homes. God's way always works. We can overcome the world, not let the world overcome us.

Men and women change through prayer. Behind every godly man is a godly woman on her knees before God. She could be a wife, daughter, mother or grandmother.

It is time for men to be the men God has created them to be—in their families and in their churches—that the body of Christ might be perfected. Men of God will build up their wives and children. Homes will be in order.

Neither husband nor wife waits for the other to act. Both know God's commands and obey as unto Him.

"And he will restore the hearts of the fathers to their children, and the hearts of the children to their fathers" (Malachi 4:6).

Chapter 25

DIVORCE AND REMARRIAGE

The divorce rate among Christians and non-Christians alike is sky-high. More and more pastors and church members face the questions that surround divorce and remarriage:

Is it ever right to divorce?

What if I were not a Christian at the time of my divorce?

What if my partner left me?

Am I allowed to remarry?

In Chapter 21 we looked at God's plan for marriage. Now let's try to gain a clearer understanding, through prayer and studying the Scriptures, of how He views divorce and remarriage.

25.1 GOD'S PERMISSIVE GROUNDS FOR DIVORCE

God hates divorce (Malachi 2:16). But because of our hardness of hearts and unwillingness to yield to Him, God does permit it on a couple of grounds.

Unchastity. "Every one who divorces his wife," Jesus said, "except for the cause of unchastity, makes her commit adultery; and whoever marries a divorced woman commits adultery" (Matthew 5:32).

God does allow divorce, then, for unchastity.

Unchastity includes any unfaithfulness, whether it be fornication—a sexual relationship outside marriage; or adultery—a sexual relationship between a married person and someone other than his or her spouse.

Fornication needs to be considered in light of ancient Jewish customs. A young woman and young man, with their parents' blessing and usually by their parents' choice, would make a commitment to one another, called a betrothal, and in some cases would sign a legally binding contract that could be broken only by divorce.

Then they separated, each one remaining in his or her parents' home, for as long as a year. During this time preparations were completed for the marriage ceremony and their future life together—establishing a financial base, obtaining a home, and the like. They were not to see one another during that time.

At the end of that period they would come back together. If there had been no sexual involvement on the part of either one during that time, the marriage would be officially consummated.

But if any sexual involvement—fornication—had occurred, it represented grounds for divorce, since the couple had made a binding commitment before God.

How different the world would be if we practiced that custom today! One application of it would be that couples set aside a time of waiting on God for His clear direction in their plans, to be sure they are following *His* plans for them. It might also strengthen their commitment to one another and help to purify their motives.

In the matter of fornication and adultery, Christians have been given the ministry of reconciliation. Sexual sin is not unforgivable. God is able to restore marriages in which adultery has occurred.

Desertion. The apostle Paul states, with regard to this second biblical grounds for divorce: "But if the unbelieving depart, let him depart. A brother or sister is not under bondage in such cases: but God hath called us to peace" (1 Corinthians 7:15, KJV).

This verse refers to a marriage between an unbeliever and a believer, when the unbeliever wants to depart. The word *bondage* in Greek is *douloo*, which means to bring into, to enslave, or to make a servant. This verse, then, translated literally, breaks these ties and makes the marriage relationship null and void in order to maintain peace. Some freedom may result when the unbeliever has departed.

Let us keep foremost in our minds that the Christian's commitment is to be open in all cases to reconciliation and restoration. Yet if either partner decides to divorce because of unchastity or desertion, certain guidelines should be followed.

25.2 COUNSEL FOR THE DIVORCED PERSON

First, all divorce action should rest primarily with the guilty party—that is, the one who deserts or is unfaithful.

Second, the innocent party should make every effort to bring about reconciliation. Would God do any less? He is a reconciler, a restorer.

Third, the innocent party should never seek a divorce without seeking sound biblical counsel and release from God.

Our counsel to one contemplating divorce must adhere to God's Word. We do not want someone to "feel good" about any action that contradicts biblical principles. So every attempt should be made to restore the marriage relationship regardless of the circumstances.

When divorce is inevitable, we can help a Christian brother or sister to find freedom from condemnation and torturing emotions, helping him or her on to a new life.

One of the greatest inadequacies of the Church is the handling of those who have experienced divorce, whatever the circumstances. We can agree with the Bible that marriage is to be a permanent relationship. But, although God can forgive someone whose marriage has ended in divorce, the Church has had difficulty forgiving him and helping him to rebuild his life.

Divorce has no winners, just bruised and battered victims. The divorced Christian seems forever branded *second-class citizen* and *unforgivable* by many in the Church. In fact, some churches do not allow divorced persons to become members.

Where can divorced Christians go for help and healing if not to the Church? The Christian community, moreover, is exhorted to love and forgive one another.

God's Word does not say that He is faithful and righteous to forgive us our sins and to cleanse us from all unrighteousness—*except for divorce.* It also does not say to be kind to one another, tenderhearted, forgiving each other—*except for the divorced person.*

No one needs love and forgiveness more than the divorced person, for divorce is the ultimate rejection, a rejection synonymous with the word unlovable.

Divorce is more traumatic than death. Death is final, but the effects of divorce can linger for a lifetime. The scars remain even after remarriage, and something will always open up the wounds of the past. No one can honestly say (unless he or she has a hardened heart), "Divorce is a breeze. It didn't affect me at all."

May we who represent the Church reach out in obedience to God's Word to our hurting brothers and sisters. May we love and forgive them as the Lord Jesus has, and help them to rebuild their lives as a testimony to a loving, forgiving, and faithful God.

A divorced person's greatest needs are to have freedom from guilt and rejection; to get rid of bitterness, resentment, and unforgiveness; and to realize his or her worth and usefulness to God and other people.

Those who suddenly become single through divorce have had part of their lives cut off. They do not seem to fit into a normal lifestyle. The Church has a responsibility to help them fit. And single parents should have the freedom to approach their elders and deacons for guidance with finances, child-rearing, emotional turmoil—in short, any need that may beset them.

25.3 CHILDREN OF DIVORCE

Parents going through a divorce are often more concerned with their own emotions than those of their children. Other parents feel helpless to give comfort because they may be experiencing guilt.

U.S. Census statistics for 1984 indicate that

single parents headed 25.7 percent of the families in the U.S. with children under 18. By 1990 single parents will head one out of every three families, possibly one out of two. And a study conducted by the Yale Child Study Center revealed that 45 percent of all children born in any given year will live with only one of their parents at some time before they are 18. Single parents in the past decade have increased by 80 percent.

Herein are potential tragedies, for each child of divorced parents is a prime target for emotional damage. Young children respond to a divorce, for example, by feeling they are responsible. Somehow they "failed" and "let" it happen. They need to realize they did not cause the divorce.

Teenagers may struggle most with torn loyalties. They love both parents and do not understand why their parents cannot work out the problems and stay together. All children may be gripped by depression, anger, low self-esteem, fear of abandonment, and loss of love. Children almost always desire reconciliation over divorce.

Parents going through divorce should impress upon their children that they love them and are not divorcing them. In some cases, increased parental dialogue with the children has even helped the parents to reconcile.

Children who become part of a step-family find it complicated and confusing, and sometimes feel they have been twice defeated. First, they could not prevent the divorce; and second, they could not prevent the remarriage.

These children need special understanding, encouragement, and direction.

25.4 GOD'S GROUNDS FOR REMARRIAGE

Just as God permits divorce on certain grounds, He also permits remarriage under certain circumstances.

Death. "A wife is bound as long as her husband lives; but if her husband is dead, she is free to be married to whom she wishes, only in the Lord" (1 Corinthians 7:39).

Those last four words are the key to remarriage: *only in the Lord,* not based on feelings, not for convenience, but as He directs.

Someone who has lost a spouse through death then has scriptural freedom to remarry. But it is best to wait at least a year, preferably two years, before doing so, allowing time and the Holy Spirit a chance to heal, strengthen, and give clear direction.

Desertion. The believing partner left behind after the unbeliever departs (see 1 Corinthians 7:15) also has some freedom to remarry, according to 1 Corinthians 7:27–28: "Art thou bound unto a wife? seek not to be loosed. Art thou loosed from a wife? seek not a wife. But and if thou marry, thou hast not sinned" (KJV).

If you remarry after being "loosed," Paul says, you have not sinned. But again, this passage seems to refer directly to one who has been scripturally released as in 1 Corinthians 7:15—on grounds of desertion. So when the unbeliever desires to depart, let him depart. And the believer is free to remarry.

Unfaithfulness. Where unfaithfulness has existed in a marriage, the innocent party is given freedom to remarry. Jesus said, "And I say to you, whoever divorces his wife, except for immorality, and marries another commits adultery" (Matthew 19:9).

In all cases in which the innocent party in a divorce contemplates remarriage, the following guidelines may be helpful.

He or she should seek to establish a marriage relationship that pleases God by first confessing and repenting any sins from the previous marriage, including the marriage vow that has been broken.

"So then if, while her husband is living, she is joined to another man, she shall be called an adulteress; but if her husband dies, she is free from the law, so that she is not an adulteress, though she is joined to another man" (Romans 7:3).

Regardless of the fact that one has been deserted, he or she must still deal with the first marriage vow, when planning to remarry, because the vow made to God is still intact. It is vital for the believer, whether he was "at fault" or not, to repent of having participated in breaking the vow in order to free himself from destructive feelings of guilt.

Second, the innocent party should not be the first to remarry so as to allow God to work out a reconciliation. Otherwise, more guilt can ensue. All attempts at reconciliation and restoration have failed when the one who left remarries. In that case there is freedom to remarry.

Third, all guilt, resentment, bitterness, or unforgiveness should be confronted before considering remarriage. There are problems enough in the new relationship without carrying that excess weight of sin from the previous marriage.

The prospective marriage mate should be a believer, one who preferably has never been married. That way, fewer problems will be brought into the new relationship. Two divorced people can bring residual problems from their previous marriages into the new relationship. Those who marry one who has never married often find strength in the new mate to help him or her through the hurts from the previous marriage. The new mate will not be able to empathize, but he can encourage.

It is also helpful for a couple to wait at least one year prior to remarriage. In that time hurts can be healed, feelings settled, and financial strains from the divorce resolved. A waiting period will also help a couple be sure they are choosing the right partner according to God's will. They can seek godly counsel that will set them on more solid footing before remarriage, and give them time to help their children adjust to the idea of a new man or woman who is to influence their life.

Again, remarriage on *any* grounds should be considered only after an individual fails at all attempts for reconciliation, and has received solid biblical counsel and God's consent and blessing. Then he may begin life afresh, for, as Scripture promises, "If any man is in Christ, he is a new creature; the old things passed away; behold, new things have come" (2 Corinthians 5:17).

V

THE
FAMILY

Restoring the Biblical Family

Parents in Perspective

Training Our Children

Wife and Child Abuse

Chapter 26

RESTORING THE BIBLICAL FAMILY

We can have success in our families only by following God's way. The biblical family prospers when the needs of spirit and soul are known and a desire exists to follow godly principles.

The Old Testament exhorts us to obey God, for in doing so He will bless us (see Deuteronomy 28:1–2). God has not changed. He rewards obedience today just as He rewarded the people of Israel when they obeyed.

26.1 THE LEADER

God has placed fathers in a crucial position. They can choose to bless their family, or to block His graces from reaching them, for a father's blessing directs the flow of God's giving.

The principles are simple. God has given us a free will. He has given parents the care of their children. The children's blessing, therefore, waits upon the parents' invitation. A child without a father's blessing wanders in a spiritually arid and fruitless land.

The power of a blessing is passed on to a family in three ways:

1. In a practical way, heredity and example give us physical health and a tendency toward good character. If parents have good health and godly character, their children most likely will, too.

2. We are blessed by a desire to excel and rise above our circumstances.

3. Whatever patterns, habits and traditions we instill will influence following generations.

By the principle of sowing and reaping, if parents bless their children, then they will bless their children after them. All this begins with a pure heart. God wants parents to have pure hearts because all that happens in their lives affects their children. "A good man leaves an inheritance to his children's children" (Proverbs 13:22a).

On the negative side, God said He would visit "the iniquity of the fathers on the children, on the third and the fourth generations of those who hate Me." More positively, He promised to show "lovingkindness to thousands, to those who love Me and keep My commandments" (see Exodus 20:5–6).

Parents need to pray daily for their children. And they will want to pray for guidance, trusting God to counsel them about their children's future. As a parent prayerfully follows God's principles of discipline, authority, and holiness, a child's spirit and soul will be nurtured. After all, holiness is not religiosity or adherence to rigid laws. It is the life of love lived out every day in the family. It is personal love, expressed personally in the home. It is obedience from the heart to God's Word.

Children are a gift from God. So let parents seek to know Him better and love Him more fully, that His life in them will have a positive effect on their children. For spiritual renewal begins in the home, as families are restored to right relationships with God.

26.2 THE FAMILY'S PROTECTION

The family is probably experiencing more turmoil and spiritual attack today than at any other time. Yet many problems can be prevented when fathers function in their God-ordained role as head of the home.

In the beginning, in the Garden of Eden, Eve failed to submit to her husband and Adam did not protect her from falling into the serpent's trap. Adam then became part of her sin, and sin entered the world. When God saw what had happened, He called out to the man, "Where are you?" (see Genesis 3:9).

If ever there was a call to men today, it is that: "Men, where are you?" God asks men, "Are you functioning as heads of your households? Are you living and teaching My Word? Are you setting a good example for your wives and children to follow?"

According to some reports, fathers spend a daily average of less than one minute with their children. If this trend continues, the enemy will succeed in destroying many families in the Church.

Fathers, therefore, need to spend quality time in training and disciplining their children, thus fulfilling their roles in protecting and leading their families to salvation. They must set a godly example, defeating the enemy's attack against their families by assuming spiritual leadership and using the authority God has given them through His Word.

God has made provision in a number of ways for a husband and father to protect his family.

Bind the Enemy. First, Satan's activities must be restricted. He goes about "like a roaring lion, seeking someone to devour" (see 1 Peter 5:8). His special target seems to be the sons and daughters in every Christian home. Every father must therefore be on the alert. As head of the home, he must bind or restrict the enemy's power.

"When a strong man fully armed guards his own homestead, his possessions are undisturbed; but when someone stronger than he attacks him and overpowers him, he takes away from him all his armor on which he had relied, and distributes his plunder" (Luke 11:21–22).

God's Word promises that "whatever you shall bind [or forbid] on earth, shall have been bound in heaven; and whatever you loose [permit] on earth shall have been loosed in heaven" (Matthew 18:18, brackets added).

Exercise Spiritual Warfare. Second, the enemy's strongholds must be destroyed. When a person establishes a pattern of sinful responses, he allows Satan to set strongholds or fortresses in his life. Even though the Lord Jesus rendered the enemy powerless by His death on the cross, the enemy holds onto any ground he has taken prior to an individual's conversion. This applies to every family member—mother, father, son, or daughter.

Husbands and fathers have the following assurance and exhortation from Scripture, which they should practice daily:

"For though we walk in the flesh, we do not war according to the flesh, for the weapons of our warfare are not of the flesh, but divinely powerful for the destruction of fortresses. We are destroying speculations and every lofty thing raised up against the knowledge of God, and we are taking every thought captive to the obedience of Christ" (2 Corinthians 10:3–5).

As fathers become acquainted with the enemy's ways, they will "resist him, firm in your faith, knowing that the same experiences of suffering are being accomplished by your brethren who are in the world" (1 Peter 5:9).

Fathers are not to give the enemy any ground. Sin exists in the first place because we entertain a sinful thought and let it gain entrance into our lives. But we must "take *every* thought captive to the obedience of Christ" at the instant it knocks on the door of our mind.

Make a Protective Hedge. Third, husbands and fathers must establish God's protective hedge about their families. In response to a godly father's actions, God protects his family in a special way. When a father faithfully fulfills his role, his children, his business, and his possessions are safe.

So fathers must develop those characteristics essential to establishing the protective hedge.

Job, a man of character living in the fear of God, had been blessed with a large family and great herds of livestock. At the outset of his Old Testament story, God and Satan are talking. Satan tells God that he has been "roaming about on the earth and walking around on it" (see Job 1:7). God asks him, "Have you considered My servant Job?" (see verse 8).

Satan replies, "Hast Thou not made a hedge about him and his house and all that he has, on every side?" (verse 10a). In other words, "No. You have him hedged in; I can't get to him."

So it was that God lifted His hand of protection, removing that hedge, so that Job might be tested. Until God lifted the hedge, Satan could not touch him.

We too experience trials and circumstances only because God allows them. Any other theology says that God is not in control and that Satan is bigger; and he is not. God is bigger and more powerful. Only what passes the hand of God—what He permits—will touch our lives.

As Job experienced severe anguish, he never denied God. He questioned Him and what He was doing, but did not deny Him. When Job took his eyes off himself and his problems, and interceded for his friends who had counseled him (somewhat unwisely), God restored his fortunes.

To make a hedge effective in his family, a father must obey God and follow His steps. And a key step, as we saw in Job, is to enter into intercessory prayer. Elsewhere God declares: "And I searched for a man among them who should build up the wall and stand in the gap before Me for the land, that I should not destroy it; but I found no one" (Ezekiel 22:30).

That is God's heart for fathers, that they will "stand in the gap" or intercede for His work in their families. Let God not say of fathers that He has found none who will pray. If a family member goes his or her own way and rebels against God, that one can be restored by the father's building a "hedge of thorns" through prayer.

To understand this hedge of thorns, let's look at the Old Testament story of Hosea and his adulterous wife, Gomer.

"For [she] has played the harlot; She . . . has acted shamefully. For she said, 'I will go after my lovers, Who give me my bread and my water, My wool and my flax, my oil and my drink.' Therefore, behold, I will hedge up her way with thorns, And I will build a wall against her so that she cannot find her paths. And she will pursue her lovers, but she will not overtake them; And she will seek them, but will not find them. Then she will say, 'I will go back to my first husband, for it was better for me then than now!' " (Hosea 2:5–7).

What happened in Gomer's life because of the hedge of thorns? She lost direction. She could not find her lovers. And she returned to her husband.

God's Word works. Fathers need to exercise this principle of the hedge of thorns by praying it around themselves, their wives, and their children. They will see results, sometimes instantly and at other times progressively.

The hedge of thorns may be needed to protect a child from himself and to protect him from peer pressure and other wrong influences, in the same way Jesus prayed for our protection: "Simon, Simon, behold, Satan has demanded permission to sift you like wheat; but I have prayed for you, that your faith may not fail; and you, when once you have turned again, strengthen your brothers" (Luke 22:31–32).

John's Gospel contains Jesus' farewell prayer for His disciples, in which Jesus shows us His love and protection: "While I was with them, I was keeping them in Thy name which Thou hast given Me; and I guarded them, and not one of them perished but the son of perdition, that the Scripture might be fulfilled" (John 17:12).

As in the example of Job, there are times when the hedge should be removed. If a child rejects the truth, a father must pray that the hedge of protection be removed to allow the Lord to carry out further discipline.

1 Corinthians 5:5 shows what Paul intended in just such a situation: "I have decided to deliver [a certain fallen brother] to Satan for the destruction of his flesh, that his spirit may be saved in the day of the Lord Jesus."

Nevertheless, we can pray and establish a "hedge of thorns" around an individual, and be sure of good results. For God never fails.

26.3 ATTRIBUTES OF A GODLY FATHER

Five character traits of a godly father can be drawn from the following passage of Scripture, in which Paul addresses the Thessalonians as a spiritual father:

"Having thus a fond affection for you, we were well-pleased to impart to you not only the gospel of God but also our own lives, because you had become very dear to us. For you recall, brethren, our labor and hardship, how working night and day so as not to be a burden to any of you, we proclaimed to you the gospel of God. You are witnesses and so is God, how devoutly and uprightly and blamelessly we behaved toward you believers; just as you know how we were exhorting and encouraging and imploring each one of you as a father would his own children, so that you may walk in a manner worthy of the God who calls you into His own kingdom and glory" (1 Thessalonians 2:8–12).

First of all, a godly father will have a *fond affection* for his family. He is a vessel of God's love for each member.

Second, he *imparts his life*. He gives his all,

being willing to lay down his life for his wife and children as Christ laid down His life for the Church. After God, a man's wife and children are more important to him than anyone else in the world.

Third, a godly father is an *example of hard work and unselfishness*. He is not sitting back waiting to be blessed, but is diligent to see that the spiritual, emotional, and physical needs of his family are being met.

Fourth, his life is a *proclamation of the gospel*. He shares the message of Christ at every opportunity, not ashamed that he follows Him.

Fifth, a godly father has an *authentic, positive Christian influence*. That is, he encourages his wife and children, spiritually and in every way. When Christ controls a man's life, that man's family and others around him will know it.

26.4 CONVICTIONS

Ten scriptural convictions have been developed from the Ten Commandments of the Old Testament. These are important for husbands and fathers to understand as they seek to fulfill their responsibilities. Every man needs to teach his family these convictions, in order to protect them from the destructive influences of wrong desires and temptations, as well as false philosophies.

1. God alone is sovereign, and the Bible is His inspired Word and the final authority for my life.

First Commandment: "Thou shalt have no other gods before me" (Exodus 20:3, KJV). To reject God's sovereignty and inspiration makes a god of my own intellect.

2. My purpose in life is to seek God with my whole heart and to build my goals around His priorities.

Second Commandment: "Thou shalt not make unto thee any graven image . . . nor serve them" (verses 4–5, KJV).

3. My body is the living temple of God and must not be defiled by the lusts of the world.

Third Commandment: "Thou shalt not take the name of the Lord thy God in vain" (verse 7, KJV). We damage His name by immorality.

4. My church must teach the foundational truths of the Bible and reinforce my basic convictions.

Fourth Commandment: "Remember the sabbath day, to keep it holy" (verse 8, KJV).

5. My children and grandchildren belong to God, and it is my responsibility to teach them scriptural principles, godly character, and basic convictions.

Fifth Commandment: "Honour thy father and thy mother" (verse 12, KJV). A child's honor permits a father to teach.

6. My activities must never weaken the scriptural convictions of another Christian.

Sixth Commandment: "Thou shalt not kill" (verse 13, KJV). When we undermine the faith of another, we are in grave danger of God's judgment.

7. My marriage is a lifelong commitment to God and to my marriage partner.

Seventh Commandment: "Thou shalt not commit adultery" (verse 14, KJV).

8. My money is a trust from God and must be earned and managed according to scriptural principles.

Eighth Commandment: "Thou shalt not steal" (verse 15, KJV).

9. My words must be in harmony with God's Word, especially when reproving and restoring a Christian brother.

Ninth Commandment: "Thou shalt not bear false witness against thy neighbour" (verse 16, KJV).

10. My affections must be set on things above, not on things on the earth.

Tenth Commandment: "Thou shalt not covet thy neighbour's house . . . nor any thing that is thy neighbour's" (verse 17, KJV).

How can a father build a conviction? 1 Corinthians 16:13–14 provides guidelines: "Be on the alert, stand firm in the faith, act like men, be strong. Let all that you do be done in love."

He should be alert to spiritual danger, know what his wife and children face each day, and not let the adversary afflict them. As Solomon urged, "Know well the condition of your flocks" (Proverbs 27:23).

Fathers must be true to God's standards, not compromising or accepting the standards of the world. God has set His standards in place so we can read and follow them; He has written them upon our hearts by His Spirit.

Fathers must be men of God, strong and bold in the Spirit, kind and loving in all that they do.

A man may excel in any one of these areas. But to be the husband and father God wants him to be, he will achieve a balance in all.

Chapter 27

PARENTS IN PERSPECTIVE

We live in a day in which societal and other pressures push us to compromise our parental roles and responsibilities.

To understand our responsibilities as parents, we must understand God's principles for the family. We have studied a godly marriage and now want to look at the role of parents through God's eyes.

27.1 CHILDREN: GOD'S BLESSINGS

"Behold, children are a gift of the Lord; The fruit of the womb is a reward. Like arrows in the hand of a warrior, so are the children of one's youth. How blessed is the man whose quiver is full of them; They shall not be ashamed, When they speak with their enemies in the gate" (Psalm 127:3–5).

God blesses parents with children. Children go through a learning process, however, and can be obnoxious and rebellious at times. Then, only through God's eyes can parents see them as a blessing from Him.

Grandparents also have a responsibility not to meddle, but to instill in their grandchildren Christlike attitudes, to encourage them, pray with them, and read the Bible with them.

The process of raising children is actually an exercise of faith, because when we entrust our children to God, we know He will keep and guard them. "I know whom I have believed," wrote Paul, "and I am convinced that He is able to guard what I have entrusted to Him until that day" (2 Timothy 1:12).

We have an opportunity to give of ourselves without limit as we care for our children unselfishly. This selfless giving helps us become more sensitive to others and to understand their needs.

Jesus taught, "Whoever wishes to become great among you shall be your servant, and whoever wishes to be first among you shall be your slave" (Matthew 20:26–27).

Our responsibility before God for our children will keep us on our knees in prayer and bring deep spiritual growth in us. As Jesus prayed for His disciples, we will pray for our families:

"I ask on their behalf; I do not ask on behalf of the world, but of those whom Thou hast given Me; for they are Thine. I do not ask Thee to take them out of the world, but to keep them from the evil one. Sanctify them in the truth; Thy word is truth" (John 17:9, 15, 17). In raising our children, we become aware of being responsible to God for the lives of others.

27.2 GOD'S PROMISES TO PARENTS

When we consider children to be a sacred trust from God, and train them to be accountable for their choices and actions, then we can trust the end result to Him. "Train up a child in the way he should go, Even when he is old he will not depart from it" (Proverbs 22:6).

We have been given several amazing promises, the first of which is that God will teach our children: "And all your sons will be taught of the Lord; And the well-being of your sons will be great" (Isaiah 54:13).

Next, our children will bless us, their parents: "Her children rise up and bless her; Her husband also, and he praises her" (Proverbs 31:28).

Parents will also receive God's approval: "His master said to him, 'Well done, good and faithful slave; you were faithful with a few things, I will put you in charge of many things; enter into the joy of your master'" (Matthew 25:23).

As we are faithful and obedient to God, what blessings He gives us!

When we respond to daily stresses in a Christlike way, and pattern our lives after the Word of God, we do more to shape our children's character than anything we say or teach. And we open the way of blessing for them.

How do parents set an example for their children?

We must make Christ a reality in our lives and show a sincere faith in Him and His promises. "For I am mindful of the sincere faith within you," wrote Paul to Timothy, "which first dwelt in your grandmother Lois, and your mother Eunice, and I am sure that it is in you as well" (2 Timothy 1:5).

We must practice what we want our children to practice: "The things you have learned and received and heard and seen in me, practice these things; and the God of peace shall be with you" (Philippians 4:9). Paul also wrote, "Be imitators of me, just as I also am of Christ" (1 Corinthians 11:1).

We should be like Christ in thought, word, and deed so that as our children grow and imitate us, they will also be like Christ. Our children should expect the very best out of us at our level of spiritual maturity. Anything less is not what God wants, nor is it a good example.

Primarily, we must respect authority. "Honor your father and your mother, that your days may be prolonged in the land which the Lord your God gives you" (Exodus 20:12). Failure to honor our parents in their God-ordained position of authority can cripple us all our lives—spiritually and perhaps even physically.

Beyond honoring parental authority, "Let every person be in subjection to the governing authorities. For there is no authority except from God, and those which exist are established by God. Therefore he who resists authority has opposed the ordinance of God; and they who have opposed will receive condemnation upon themselves" (Romans 13:1–2).

Whatever authority is placed over us, whether it be spiritual or worldly, God has ordained it. We have no excuse, therefore, for rebellion. "Rebellion is as the sin of witchcraft" (1 Samuel 15:23, KJV).

Whether or not we understand authority, we are to respect and obey it. God will take care of the inadequacies of authority. He will turn the hearts of kings (see Proverbs 21:1) and presidents. That is His responsibility. When we honor and respect our parents, respect the authority of the land and those over us in spiritual matters, and above all do not rebel against God, we set a godly example for our children to follow.

27.3 PARENTS' RESPONSIBILITY
TO DISCIPLINE

Correcting children with God's love confronts their rebellious sin nature and develops godly character. Of that much, most parents are well aware.

But before disciplining a child, we should distinguish between irresponsible or immature behavior and defiance or rebellion. Just because a child does something wrong, a spanking may not be required. An irresponsible or immature child needs teaching and a defiant or rebellious child needs discipline. We must let our children know their boundaries before enforcing discipline. And parents must agree with one another in how to discipline.

The responsibility of disciplining and training the children lies mainly with the father. The mother, of course, is to correct the children and support her husband. "Correct your son, and he will give you comfort; he will also delight your soul" (Proverbs 29:17). Also, "He who spares his rod hates his son, But he who loves him disciplines him diligently" (Proverbs 13:24). The world says the opposite.

God loves us when He disciplines us. That's how we know He loves us. (See Hebrews 12:8-11.) Our trials and testings are one way God corrects us. He takes us through tough times to expose and work out our rebellion. The same principle should apply to our children.

"Do not hold back discipline from the child; Although you beat him with the rod, he will not die. You shall beat him with the rod, And deliver his soul from Sheol" (Proverbs 23:13-14).

Parents need to be balanced and consistent in their discipline. When we are on-again-off-again, it confuses children, and indicates a similar pattern in our relationship with God.

Parents should set consistent limits in five areas: family, church, play, school, and study. When a child moves outside those limits, a parent's responsibility, according to the Bible, is to discipline. Parents should reassure their children of their love and teach them after each confrontation. The control of our children must be balanced with God's love. Children want to be disciplined; they want direction and to know their parents love and care for them.

We must not overcorrect our children (correct them in unnecessary ways), provoke them to anger, or cause them to be discouraged. "Fathers, do not exasperate your children, that they may not lose heart" (Colossians 3:21). Note the emphasis on the fathers. If there is no discipline or spirituality in the home, it is not the mother's fault. It is the father's responsibility. (See Ephesians 6:4.)

Never discipline in anger; action controls the will. Anger does not motivate our children to obedience; it only wounds their spirit. God has given us the responsibility of being parents in order to break the will of our children, not their spirit. "The spirit of a man can endure his sickness, But a broken spirit who can bear?" (Proverbs 18:14).

Likewise, it is damaging to threaten our children and then not follow through. When we make a commitment we must stand by it. "A righteous man who walks in his integrity," King Solomon wrote, "How blessed are his sons after him" (Proverbs 20:7; see also Ecclesiastes 5:5).

Discipline as God disciplines, for the good of the child, and to communicate God's holiness and love.

" 'My son, do not regard lightly the discipline of the Lord, nor faint when you are reproved by Him; For those whom the Lord loves He disciplines, And He scourges every son whom He receives.' Furthermore, we had earthly fathers to discipline us, and we respected them; shall we not much rather be subject to the Father of spirits, and live? For they disciplined us for a short time as seemed best to them, but He disciplines us for our good, that we may share His holiness" (Hebrews 12:5–6, 9–10).

Discipline as an act of love brings us into holiness and Christlikeness. (See Proverbs 3:12; 19:18; 22:15; Galatians 4:1–2.)

27.4 TRAINING CHILDREN

How are parents to train their children? First, we are to train them from God's Word:

"And these words, which I am commanding you today, shall be on your heart; and you shall teach them diligently to your sons and shall talk of them when you sit in your house and when you walk by the way and when you lie down and when you rise up" (Deuteronomy 6:6–7; see also Genesis 18:19; Deuteronomy 4:5–10; 11:19; Psalm 78:5–8.)

Second, we are to train our children as God does: "And, fathers, do not provoke your children to anger; but bring them up in the discipline and instruction of the Lord" (Ephesians 6:4).

Third, we are to train them by example: "Be imitators of me, just as I also am of Christ"

(1 Corinthians 11:1). We are not to expect something of our children that we ourselves are not doing. How often have we said, "Son, don't do as I do; do as I say"? That is not a biblical statement. They need to see in us the same qualities and actions we desire from them.

27.5 BUILDING CHARACTER

We should, first of all, dedicate our children to God before birth. From the moment of conception, while still in the womb, parents can read the Bible, pray, and sing spiritual songs to their baby. For God consecrated Jeremiah in the womb (see Jeremiah 1:5), and called Isaiah from his mother's womb (see Isaiah 44:2, 24; 49:1, 5).

Children's ages of accountability are in God's hands, but it is up to us to spend time communicating His Word to them as early as possible (from conception and birth), building character in them, and letting them see the Word at work in us. We establish a pattern for our children, either to walk in the ways of God, or to reject His ways.

Here, we are speaking about living the godly life, because our children's character reflects our character: "Behold, every one who quotes proverbs will quote this proverb concerning you, saying, 'Like mother, like daughter'" (Ezekiel 16:44).

The first privilege we have as parents is to instill in our children faith. When our faith is great and we trust in the Lord, miracles happen in our children. God honors a parent's faith. "Then Jesus answered and said to her, 'O woman, your faith is great; be it done for you as you wish.' And her daughter was healed at once" (Matthew 15:28).

And as Jesus interceded for us, we are to intercede for our children (see John 17:9–17), building the protective hedge of prayer around them.

Chapter 28

TRAINING OUR CHILDREN

Let's look briefly at the role of children in a Christian family.

28.1 BASIC TRAINING

Children need to be trained in the home according to godly principles. This is the parents' responsibility, as discussed earlier. Failure to do so will lead to rebellion, for which God will hold us accountable.

Children are to honor their father and mother. This commandment was so important that the apostle Paul underscored it in one of his letters: "Honor your father and mother (which is the first commandment with a promise), That it may be well with you, and that you may live long on the earth" (Ephesians 6:2–3).

Children are also commanded to obey their parents: "Children, be obedient to your parents in all things, for this is well-pleasing to the Lord" (Colossians 3:20).

Children should listen to their parents' instruction. Proverbs contains many wise sayings for parents in raising children, and for children in listening to their parents' counsel, such as: "Hear, my son, your father's instruction, And do not forsake your mother's teaching; Indeed, they are a graceful wreath to your head, And ornaments about your neck" (Proverbs 1:8–9; see also Proverbs 4:1–27; 6:20).

Children should also set a godly example that will touch other lives. "It is by his deeds that a lad distinguishes himself If his conduct is pure and right" (Proverbs 20:11).

Children need to understand the purpose of discipline, which only we as parents can explain:

"It is for discipline that you endure; God deals with you as with sons; for what son is there whom his father does not discipline? But if you are without discipline, of which all have become partakers, then you are illegitimate children and not sons. . . . He disciplines us for our good, that we may share His holiness. All discipline for the moment seems not to be joyful, but sorrowful; yet to those who have been trained by it, afterwards it yields the peaceful fruit of righteousness" (Hebrews 12:7–11).

As children mature in fulfilling their responsibilities, they will mature in their relationships with God, their parents, their friends, and others.

28.2 ROOTS OF REBELLION

Rebellion in children is promoted primarily by parents who have failed to function in their God-ordained responsibilities. A Gallup survey conducted in 1984 indicated that the main failures parents exhibit in the raising of their children are as follows:

1. No child discipline
2. Parents too lenient
3. Children having it too easy
4. Children neglected

5. Children unattended
6. Parents setting a poor example
7. Children not treated as persons
8. Children given too little responsibility

The above failures indicate a lack of godly love for the children, which produces in them a state of frustration, lack of purpose, lack of direction, and hopelessness. And in a Gallup youth survey, also conducted in 1984, it was revealed that the top teenage problems are drug and alcohol abuse, unemployment, and peer pressure.

The lack of parental concern and involvement has further fostered many root problems in our children leading to their rebellion. The most prevalent are as follows:

Sibling Rivalry. This is caused by a child's basic sin nature motivated by self-preservation, and can be promoted by parents who favor one child over another.

Peer Pressure. The force of peer pressure is operable in a child's life because of his need for acceptance among those of his own age group. Yielding to peer pressure only prolongs the development of a positive self image and promotes the rejection of parental authority, resulting in a negative outlook on the future and distrust of the same peers from whom he sought acceptance. Yielding to peer pressure is promoted by parents when they fail to provide the loving leadership, training, security, encouragement, and acceptance that a child needs to stand alone against tides of popular opinion.

Abusive Language. Hostile or vulgar language is an indication of deep inner frustrations. Many times this habit pattern is nurtured by patterns set in the home, or picked up through peers. One of the main causes of this habit is the desire to gain attention.

Abusive Behavior.　The child who exhibits abusive behavior has been abused himself, either physically, mentally, or emotionally.

Undisciplined Lifestyle / Laziness.　Slothfulness is encouraged by parents who lack discipline in their own lives. The opposite may also be true: when a parent's expectations are unrealistic, the child may become discouraged and give up.

Ungratefulness.　When parents and peers give too much and expect too little, selfishness and ungratefulness are the result.

Refusal to Do Chores.　This may be a test of the parents' leadership and authority. If there is improper follow-through and discipline, the child will continue to rebel.

Refusal To Do Homework.　Such behavior displays a lack of discipline and purpose. Many times this is a result of the parents' failure to set priorities properly and showing little interest in the learning process.

Lying.　In most cases children have been lied to by parents and friends. This sets an ungodly pattern into motion.

Theft.　The child who steals has generally been stolen from. The attention, love, and acceptance he needs have been lacking and he feels like the victim of a robbery.

Sexual Sins. Many sexual sins result from a lack of parental love and acceptance, causing a desire to gratify the flesh.

Drug and Alcohol Abuse. Such destructive behavior can be motivated by peer pressure, parental example, and a desire to escape the realities of life.

28.3 GENERAL GUIDELINES

It is helpful to establish some general guidelines for parents faced with these areas of manifested rebellion in their children.

Sibling Rivalry. Each child should be made to feel that his position in the family is unique and special in God's sight. The recognition and development of talents and gifts is a valuable tool in accomplishing this. "For where jealousy and selfish ambition exist, there is disorder and every evil thing" (James 3:16).

Peer Pressure. A child's greatest defense against yielding to peer pressure is his personal relationship with Jesus Christ and his ability to stand alone. The example that the parents set by not "keeping up with the Joneses" accomplishes more than any words. "Don't let the world around you squeeze you into its own mould, but let God re-mould your minds from within" (Romans 12:2, Phillips).

Abusive Language. When abusive language is prompted by what has been heard in the home, the problem rests with the sources of the offense. They must repent and ask forgiveness of the Lord and the child. When the source is outside the home, the teaching of scriptural principles regarding the tongue, along with Scripture memorization, can help to correct the abusive language problem. "Let no unwholesome word proceed from your mouth, but only such a word as is good for edification according to the need of the moment, that it may give grace to those who hear" (Ephesians 4:29).

Abusive Behavior. When abusive behavior is habitual, the parent needs to seek carefully for the underlying cause. The inner frustrations of the child need to be ministered to first before discipline is administered. "And we urge you, brethren, admonish the unruly" (1 Thessalonians 5:14).

Undisciplined Lifestyle / Laziness. What appears on the surface to be laziness may be an indication of underlying problems. Lack of proper rest, poor diet, rapid growth (especially in young teenagers), even sight and hearing problems may cause a child to manifest little motivation. When the cause is a poor parental example or too high expectations, the parent must deal with his own sin. Otherwise, a schedule of work and a reward system for prompt performance can often reverse the laziness cycle. "The soul of the sluggard craves and gets nothing" (Proverbs 13:4).

Ungratefulness. A climate of gratefulness can be established in the home as parents make the children aware of all that God has done and is doing in their lives. Recognizing God as the source of all gifts develops the heart attitude of gratefulness. "But godliness actually is a means of great gain, when accompanied by contentment" (1 Timothy 6:6).

Refusal to Do Home Chores. Assisting in chores teaches a child the value of teamwork and the acceptance and fulfillment of assigned responsibilities. When a child challenges his parents' authority, the parents need to respond immediately with discipline that is appropriate to the defiant act. Many times the example of parents in the home does not encourage the child to fulfill his responsibilities. The parents need to confess and repent of their failure to set a godly example for their child to follow. "For even when we were with you, we used to give you this order: If anyone will not work, neither let him eat" (2 Thessalonians 3:10).

Refusal to Do Homework. The priority of homework being completed before time for recreation needs to be established. This requires watchful discipline on the part of the parents, plus the exercise of responsibility for completed tasks on the part of the child. "The hand of the diligent will rule" (Proverbs 12:24).

Lying. Parents must be careful that they themselves tell the whole truth and nothing but the truth. When you are guiltless, you can then deal with the guilty. Passing over what you know is a lie because of the fear of confrontation only increases the problem. Make truth the standard of your home regardless of the cost. "Therefore, laying aside falsehood, speak truth, each one of you, with his neighbor, for we are members of one another" (Ephesians 4:25).

Theft. The item taken must be returned; the child must state that it was stolen; and he must request forgiveness from God and the person from whom he stole it. If the item has been destroyed or damaged, it must be replaced by the child from his own earnings. Parents should use this situation to teach the child about ownership. Reinforce with Scripture and ask the child to express how he would feel if someone stole something from him. Ask the child if there is any way in which he feels that he has been "stolen from" (your time or interest, for example). Then respond as God would have you respond through forgiveness and change. "Jesus said, 'You shall not commit murder; You shall not commit adultery; You shall not steal; You shall not bear false witness'" (Matthew 19:18.)

Sexual Sins.   When natural curiosity about sex is not directed to a knowledge of God's purposes for it, sexual indiscretions result. Parents should help the young person to understand the value of holy living, thus directing his energies to godly pursuits. The example of parents who love one another and display affection helps to bring balance into the young person's understanding of the proper place of sex. "Because it is written, 'You shall be holy, for I am holy'" (1 Peter 1:16).

Drug and Alcohol Abuse.   When a child desires alcohol or drugs, it is to escape from reality. The parents need to determine what is motivating this desire. Many times outside help from a trained counselor may reveal that the parents are not fulfilling their godly responsibilities toward the child. A parent may also be dependent upon alcohol or drugs, thereby setting a sin pattern in motion for the child. That parent needs to seek deliverance through confessing and repenting of his sin. "And do not get drunk with wine, for that is dissipation, but be filled with the Spirit" (Ephesians 5:18).

All these manifestations of rebellion in a child's life are signposts saying, "Please help me. Give me some direction."

"So then each one of us shall give account of himself to God" (Romans 14:12).

During adolescence a child is controlled by his base nature of sin and the reflective example of his parents. The age of accountability is that time in the life of a child when he comes to an understanding of what sin (rebellion) is in his life and accepts Jesus Christ. At that time, he is accountable to God for dealing with the rebellion manifested in his life.

I believe the age of accountability in a child's life depends on the Christlike example a parent projects to the child, and the discipline and training that child receives in the home. This bears directly on how soon that child receives Christ.

It is our God-given responsibility to respond in the training and discipline of our children, setting a life testimony for them to follow. "Train up a child in the way he should go, Even when he is old he will not depart from it" (Proverbs 22:6). "And these words, which I am commanding you today, shall be on your heart; and you shall teach them diligently to your sons and shall talk of them when you sit in your house and when you walk by the way and when you lie down and when you rise up" (Deuteronomy 6:6–7).

In recognizing and accepting our responsibilities as parents, what can we do to correct our failures of the past? We must first confess to God our sin of failing as a parent, and receive His forgiveness. Next, we must ask our children to forgive us, and set ourselves upon a new path of godly parenting.

28.4 DON'T'S AND DO'S

Don't's:

Praise only for achievements. Your child may feel: "What I produce and achieve is more important than who I am as a person. If I don't keep producing, no one can possibly love me or accept me."

Set perfection as a criterion for acceptance. Your child may feel: "I am inadequate and unloved, a failure, if I make any mistakes at all and don't maintain a standard of perfection in everything I do."

Discuss a child's failure to measure up to others. Your child may feel: "I am not as capable as my peers, and I must always work extra hard to make up for my deficiencies, if I want to feel good about myself."

Tell your children how hard you had it growing up, or how easy they have it, or how little they appreciate. Rather, help them learn values.

Turn every discussion into a monologue about finances. That communicates that the main thing you value is money.

Instill a negative or critical perception of other people.

Do's:

Accept unconditionally. To be effective, this kind of parental response should not be attached to any kind of accomplishment. It is sad to realize how many successful adults grow to maturity with deep feelings of inadequacy because their parents did not communicate unconditional acceptance during development. "Wherefore, accept one another, just as Christ also accepted us to the glory of God" (Romans 15:7).

Recognize each achievement. Respond to what the child has done well, not to what could have been done better. Do not compare him with other children. And support children through setbacks and failures. "Therefore encourage one another, and build up one another, just as you also are doing" (1 Thessalonians 5:11).

Make play or leisure experiences times of relaxation by slowing down and enjoying the process of experiencing, and not just the outcome. Many parents have developed a bad habit of working at leisure, which sets a poor example for children. Teach them always to respect others, to focus on their strengths, and to maintain a solidly optimistic personal viewpoint on life and living. "Here is what I have seen to be good and fitting: to eat, to drink and enjoy oneself in all one's labor in which he toils under the sun during the few years of his life which God has given him; for this is his reward" (Ecclesiastes 5:18).

Touch each of your children affectionately every day. Children need affectionate touching from parents for healthy development. "And beyond all these things put on love, which is the perfect bond of unity" (Colossians 3:14).

Learn to solve problems and conflicts in healthy ways. A true source of pride in parenting is for you to be modeled later by your children, not rejected for all you stand for. "Let no one look down on your youthfulness, but rather in speech, conduct, love, faith and purity, show yourself an example of those who believe" (1 Timothy 4:12).

Set and enforce limits for your children. Your relationship with your child almost always improves when you set reasonable limits and enforce them consistently. There is no better way to love your child than to take the time for caring discipline. "For those whom the Lord loves He disciplines . . . All discipline for the moment seems not to be joyful, but sorrowful; yet to those who have been trained by it, afterwards it yields the peaceful fruit of righteousness" (Hebrews 12:6, 11).

Teach your children work responsibilities. Recent evidence clearly indicates that children who had chores and other family responsibilities during development are better adjusted and more successful as adults. Through such activities, the child learns the realistic relationship between effort and reward, and begins to adopt healthy work habits. It is easy to give your children all you did not have as a child, but it is a mistake you both will pay for later. "And these words, which I am commanding you today, shall be on your heart; and you shall teach them diligently to your sons and shall talk of them when you sit in your house and when you walk by the way and when you lie down and when you rise up" (Deuteronomy 6:6–7).

Eat a meal together daily. It is surprising how many busy families are never all together, for even a few moments from week to week. It is a sad statement that one meal may be virtually the only opportunity for sharing with one another as a family on a daily basis. Make this minimum time together a must. "And let us consider how to stimulate one another to love and good deeds, not forsaking our own assembling together" (Hebrews 10:24–25).

Always be there for your children when there is a problem, hurt feelings, or emotional upset. Being there means supportive caring and helping in a positive way. It is also important for you to participate in the special events and milestones of your child's life. By caring enough to be there for each child, you help build a strong self-concept and an inner security that would not otherwise be possible. Treat your children as your greatest legacy, because that is just what they are.

Keep in mind that your children must grow up in a world far more complex and difficult than the days of your own youth. Take the time to be involved and to know each of your children deeply. They need all the help they can get. You will benefit, too. Your children are naturally loving and their feelings for you will grow deeper and stronger and more fulfilling unless you systematically stamp them out with cynicism, inaccessibility, and neglect of their emotional needs. "But encourage one another day after day, as long as it is still called 'Today,' lest any one of you be hardened by the deceitfulness of sin" (Hebrews 3:13).

Material content used by permission from Dr. Bruce A. Baldwin of "Direction Dynamics," author of the book *It's All in Your Head: Lifestyle Management Strategies for Busy People!*

Chapter 29

WIFE AND
CHILD ABUSE

29.1 WIFE ABUSE

Each year 28 million American women suffer the anguish of abuse. Not all abuse is physical. Some of the most harmful is emotional, leaving wounds that can take years to heal. In 65 to 90 percent of all American marriages, physical force is used at least once.

Why would a man beat the woman he has vowed to love and cherish? Why would a man who claims to be a Christian yield to such violent behavior?

Abusive husbands are men who hurt and who have not yet learned to cope with the stresses of life. Physical or emotional problems, alcohol or drug abuse may cause—but not excuse—a man's uncontrolled temper.

Sadly, an abusive man will often convince his wife that *she* is to blame for his violent outbursts. He feels he has the right to punish her, and will continue his abuse as long as he is allowed to blame his wife.

An abusive husband must be helped to accept responsibility for his own actions and turn to God for daily strength to overcome his abusive nature. The violence will never end unless one or both partners decide to do something about it, and then stick to the decision.

This may involve separation while both individuals receive intensive personal counseling, followed by several months of marriage counseling.

29.2 HELP FOR THE ABUSIVE HUSBAND

A separation of four to six months may be necessary for the wife's safety, as well as for the husband to consider his situation and gain control of his actions. Before and during the separation the husband needs to seek biblical counseling, in which he must be helped to confront his violent behavior, and purpose to change.

Reconciliation between husband and wife should be the goal of the counselor and the couple. A major step toward this is for the husband to confess and repent of the sin of anger, and then ask forgiveness of God and his wife and children.

Above all, he must be counseled to make Jesus Lord of his life. (See Chapter 3, Guiding Someone to Christ.)

29.3 HELP FOR THE ABUSED WIFE

The abused wife needs to understand how she became involved in the abuse cycle. For her sake and her husband's, she must forgive him and seek to change any words or actions that may have contributed to the cycle.

Family and friends of the couple should encourage them to reconcile. A vital part in reconciliation is counseling with both partners. But before any counsel can be effective, or any attempt be made at reconciliation of the marriage, the abusive husband must be willing to change.

When violence goes unchecked, an abused wife

should file charges with legal authorities. Yet few women take that step. Since most families depend on the man's income, the wife may be afraid that her husband will be sent to jail, curtailing income for herself and her children. While this is a real issue to be faced, the fear should not control her.

Neither should an abused wife be controlled by her fear of the husband's return. Most cities have abuse shelters. A quick call to the police will usually supply a woman with a hot-line number. She needs to get in touch with people who can help her. If she presses charges, a counselor from the shelter will usually be assigned to help her through the court proceedings.

29.4 HEALING FOR THE ABUSED WIFE

The abused wife will also want to take certain steps for her emotional healing.

She needs to seek wise biblical counsel regarding her relationship with her husband. She must be willing to resolve any unforgiveness, bitterness, and resentment she may have toward her husband. The wounds are deep, but with the help and comfort of the Holy Spirit, as well as godly counsel, she can be restored to emotional wholeness.

If she has children, they should also seek biblical counsel to try to correct the damage from living in a home controlled by violence.

As part of the healing process, the family must become active in a loving, Bible-believing, Christ centered church where they can be surrounded with love—an active love that is willing to help with any and all practical needs.

29.5 PREVENTIVE MEASURES

How can a woman spot tendencies of a potentially abusive man? She should ask herself the following questions:

Does he try to limit or control my relationships with other people?

Is he intensely jealous of me?

Does he control his temper?

Is there a history of violence in his family?

Does he treat me with respect?

Was his childhood a happy experience?

Does he have a healthy, spontaneous relationship with his parents?

Do we share similar goals, especially concerning our Christian commitment?

Does he use alcohol and or drugs?

Is he a homosexual?

If any of these abusive signs are present in a man, the woman should seek help for herself and her husband before violence erupts.

Many psychologists, psychiatrists, psychotherapists, and counselors agree that an abusive relationship can be healed. But it can come about only through both husband and wife being deeply committed to a healthy marriage and relying wholly on the Lord Jesus Christ, who has sovereign authority to break every cycle of sin.

29.6 CHILD ABUSE

In 1984 an alarming two million cases of child abuse were reported. According to a report from the National Center on Child Abuse and Neglect, child abuse is the leading cause of death in children under the age of 15.

Child abusers generally suffer from low self-esteem, self-hatred, fear of rejection, and a low tolerance for frustration. They are ordinary people trapped in a stressful life situation beyond their control or ability to tolerate it.

In his book *Love Must Be Tough,* Dr. James C. Dobson reports that sixty percent of all abusive parents were abused as children. Child abuse results from a breakdown in the family unit and in the individual character of the abusive parent. Offenders are found in every socioeconomic, religious, and ethnic group.

29.7 TYPES OF CHILD ABUSE

Child abuse falls into four basic categories: physical abuse, emotional abuse, sexual abuse, and neglect.

Physical. This kind of abuse is so widespread that health care professionals are required to report all suspected cases to the authorities. This type will produce bruises, lacerations, burns, or fractures in the child's body, depending on the severity of the abuse.

Emotional. This abuse may appear in children who are emotionally or physically different from other children, or who are unduly afraid of their parents.

Emotionally abused victims may cry at inappropriate times or become excessively fearful, aggressive, destructive, depressed, passive, or withdrawn. The child may have untreatable learning problems or be habitually truant. Other signs include a reluctance to return home, constant fatigue, loss of appetite, refusal to eat, or obesity.

Sexual. This abuse is harder to identify. Victims of sexual exploitation, molestation, and incest normally feel too helpless and guilty to reveal their plight.

It has been suggested that as many as one out of four children may be victims of incest (1981 statistic, according to Rachel Johnson, cited in *Transformation of the Inner Man,* by John and Paula Sanford). Dr. Dobson cites that as many as 20 to 25 percent of all women in the country were sexually abused as children.

The Bible forbids such practices: "No one is to approach any close relative to have sexual relations" (Leviticus 18:6, NIV; see also 1 Corinthians 5:1–13.)

Neglect. This kind of abuse may show up by injuries treated inadequately, frequent sickness, inappropriate dress, lack of cleanliness, frequently expressed hunger, and lack of parental supervision.

Child abuse is an evil to be abhorred. It is emotionally, psychologically, mentally, and spiritually destructive. Abuse wounds a child's spirit, and therefore requires counseling and encouragement in order for him to be healed in spirit and soul.

Known child abuse cases should be reported at once to the local authorities and social service agencies for follow-up.

29.8 HELP FOR THE CHILD ABUSER

Child abusers who are unbelievers need to recognize their sin and accept Jesus Christ as Lord and Savior. "Believe in the Lord Jesus, and you shall be saved, you and your household" (Acts 16:31).

A believer must also recognize child abuse as sin and confess and forsake it. "If we confess our sins, He is faithful and righteous to forgive us our sins and to cleanse us from all unrighteousness" (1 John 1:9).

For complete healing, the abusive person must ask forgiveness of God and the victim. And he must be filled with the Holy Spirit so as to gain control of this life-dominating problem. "Do not get drunk with wine, for that is dissipation, but be filled with the Spirit" (Ephesians 5:18).

We should refer a child abuser to a local pastor or to the appropriate professional person for counseling.

29.9 HELP FOR THE ABUSED CHILD

The child abuse victim has been shamed, and will suffer from rejection, guilt, low self-esteem, poor self-image, anger, bitterness, resentment, fear, and a deep sense of being beyond forgiveness. The victim needs understanding, prayerful support from family and friends, sound biblical counseling, and the assurance that this experience, like all experiences in life can be overcome and transformed through Christ.

They must also confess and repent of any bitterness, resentment and unforgiveness that they might have toward the abuser (see 1 John 1:9).

For complete healing, the victim *must* be encouraged to express inner feelings; only then will he be able to truly forgive the abuser. He will be released in turn from the turmoil that will otherwise dominate his emotions for life.

With the gentle help and comfort of the Holy

Spirit, the child abuse victim needs to be assured that God truly loves him, and that he is not "dirty" in God's eyes, but free of blame.

Further help should be encouraged by referring the abused child to a local pastor or Christian professional trained in this area.

VI

THE
SPIRIT
OF
ANTICHRIST

Knowing God's Spirit

Cults

Sorcery and the Occult

Deliverance

Chapter 30

KNOWING GOD'S SPIRIT

The Bible tells us that "in later times some will fall away from the faith, paying attention to deceitful spirits and doctrines of demons" (1 Timothy 4:1).

Demonic powers are real, but Christians have authority over them. Those who know God's Spirit will be better equipped to confront the spirits of darkness. We fall into all kinds of unfortunate circumstances because we do not test and try the spirits to see whether they are of God.

1 John 4:1 instructs us: "Beloved, do not believe every spirit, but test the spirits to see whether they are from God; because many false prophets have gone out into the world." God's Word is clear: Do not believe every spirit. God wants us to test the spirits by filtering them through His Holy Spirit who dwells within us.

"By this you know the Spirit of God: every spirit that confesses that Jesus Christ has come in the flesh is from God; and every spirit that does not confess Jesus is not from God; and this is the spirit of the antichrist, of which you have heard that it is coming, and now it is already in the world" (1 John 4:2–3).

How do we test and try the spirits? The following questions will help to determine the spiritual source behind another person's words or actions: *Does the person confess that Jesus Christ is the Messiah; that He is really God in human flesh?*

"[God] desires all men to be saved and to come to the knowledge of the truth. For there is one God, and one mediator also between God and men, the man Christ Jesus, who gave Himself as a ransom for all, the testimony borne at the proper time" (1 Timothy 2:4–6; see also John 1:14.)

Does he agree with God's Word?

"We are from God; he who knows God listens to us; he who is not from God does not listen to us. By this we know the spirit of truth and the spirit of error" (1 John 4:6.)

Is God's love present within him?

"Beloved, let us love one another, for love is from God; and every one who loves is born of God and knows God. The one who does not love does not know God, for God is love" (1 John 4:7–8).

Does he accept the blood atonement of Jesus Christ?

"But if we walk in the light as He Himself is in the light, we have fellowship with one another, and the blood of Jesus His Son cleanses us from all sin" (1 John 1:7).

Is God's Spirit within him?

"By this we know that we abide in Him and He in us, because He has given us of His Spirit" (1 John 4:13).

Does he confess Jesus as Savior and the Son of God?

"And we have beheld and bear witness that the Father has sent the Son to be the Savior of the world. Whoever confesses that Jesus is the Son of God, God abides in him, and he in God" (1 John 4:14–15).

Does he confess Jesus as Lord?

"No one speaking by the Spirit of God says, 'Jesus is accursed'; and no one can say, 'Jesus is Lord,' except by the Holy Spirit" (1 Corinthians 12:3).

The Holy Spirit Himself will guide us into all truth, for truth and reality come from the Holy Spirit. "But when He, the Spirit of truth, comes, He will guide you into all the truth; for He will not speak on His own initiative, but whatever He hears, He will speak; and He will disclose to you what is to come" (John 16:13).

Because God's Spirit dwells within our spirit or heart, we know Him. "For to us God revealed [these things] through the Spirit; for the Spirit searches all things, even the depths of God" (1 Corinthians 2:10; see also John 14:26.)

Chapter 31

CULTS

With God's Spirit dwelling within us, we can test the spirits and determine which are of truth and which of error.

Sometimes we may encounter a group we suspect of being a cult. A common thread in cults is that they deny the deity of Jesus Christ. They say He was a good man, a good teacher, or a good prophet, but not God revealed in the flesh, as the Bible teaches.

To help determine whether a group is a cult, we can check its operations and theology against the ten questions below. Answering yes to any of these questions does not prove that group is a cult. But considered together, the questions should stimulate our thinking and cause us to take a second look at the group.

31.1 IDENTIFYING A CULT

Does it narrow your options? Cults frequently claim that they alone have the one true faith and that everyone else is wrong.

Do the members attack a common scapegoat? Cults often try to find an enemy in a major denomination as a hate symbol. Or they may attack doctrines such as baptism, communion, marriage, or the Trinity.

Is the group rigidly structured? Does it have a leader, a pecking order, or especially a "teaching order" to ensnare minds?

Does the group rely heavily on one section of the Bible or on certain books that they alone publish and insist are important? Scriptural balance is vital for a healthy Christian life, rather than the ability to influence or pressure others with verses taken out of context.

Does the group shut off outside ideas, claiming they are wrong or sinful, and insist upon memorization of rote or canned answers?

Does the group make you feel free in your relationship with God? If not, be careful. When you are free in Christ, you are free indeed.

Does the group insist on discipline? On mandatory attendance at meetings? On continual immersion in their books, tapes, and teachings?

Does the group interfere with the normal function of your family life? If so, be careful!

Does the group make its participants happy, or sad and fearful, despite the words they speak publicly? God does not steal joy; only the thief does. (See John 10:10.)

Does the group force a person to choose between one's "beliefs" and one's husband, wife, or closest family member? God joins people together in marriage. Anything that strikes at the family unit is highly suspect.

We should not accuse every group or denomination with which we disagree of cultic behavior. Nor should we assume something is wrong with our own church if three or four of the above questions have answers that create some misgivings. Rather, we should be cautious and test the spirits according to Scripture and the Holy Spirit.

The following table compares the truth of the Bible, God's Word, with the views of various cults concerning the Godhead, Jesus Christ, the Holy Spirit, sin, salvation, and death.

31.2 GOD'S WORD VS. CULTIC BELIEFS
The Bible—the Word of God

GODHEAD	JESUS CHRIST	HOLY SPIRIT
God is a Trinity of three distinct Persons. The Father is God: "But to us there is but one God, the Father, of whom are all things, and we in him; and one Lord Jesus Christ, by whom are all things, and we by him" (1 Corinthians 8:6, KJV). The Son is God: "In the beginning was the Word, and the Word was with God, and the Word was God. The same was in the beginning with God. All things were made by him; and without Him was not any thing made that was made" (John 1:1-3, KJV). The Holy Spirit is God: "But Peter said, Ananias, why hath Satan filled thine heart to lie to the Holy Ghost, and to keep back part of the price of the land? . . . Thou hast not lied unto men, but unto God" (Acts 5:3-4, KJV). God is infinite, eternal, and unchangeable (see Romans 8:35-39; 1:20; 1:23).	Christ is God (see "Godhead"). Christ was man: "For there is one God, and one mediator between God and men, the man Christ Jesus" (1 Timothy 2:5, KJV). He is the Incarnation: "And the Word was made flesh, and dwelt among us, (and we beheld his glory, the glory as of the only begotten of the Father) full of grace and truth" (John 1:14, KJV). See also Romans 1:3; Isaiah 7:14; John 4:1-4; Hebrews 2:11-14. Christ died for mankind's sins: "Who his own self bare our sins in his own body on the tree" (1 Peter 2:24a, KJV).	See under "Godhead": The Holy Spirit is God. "But Peter said, Ananias, why hath Satan filled thine heart to lie to the Holy Ghost . . ." (Acts 5:3, KJV). The Holy Spirit is Helper, Teacher, Spirit of Truth: "But the Helper, the Holy Spirit, whom the Father will send in My name, He will teach you all things, and bring to your remembrance all that I said to you" (John 14:26). "And in the same way the Spirit also helps our weakness; for we do not know how to pray as we should, but the Spirit Himself intercedes for us with groanings too deep for words" (Romans 8:26).

The Bible—the Word of God

SIN	SALVATION	DEATH
"For all have sinned and fall short of the glory of God" (Romans 3:23). "The wages of sin is death, but the free gift of God is eternal life in Christ Jesus our Lord" (Romans 6:23). "If we say we have no sin, we are deceiving ourselves, and the truth is not in us. If we confess our sins, He is faithful and righteous to forgive us our sins and to cleanse us from all unrighteousness" (1 John 1:8–9).	"If you confess with your mouth Jesus as Lord, and believe in your heart that God raised Him from the dead, you shall be saved" (Romans 10:9). "Be it known unto you all, and to all the people of Israel, that by the name of Jesus Christ of Nazareth, whom ye crucified, whom God raised from the dead, even by him doth this man stand here before you whole. This is the stone which was set at nought of you builders, which is become the head of the corner. Neither is there salvation in any other: for there is none other name under heaven given among men, whereby we must be saved" (Acts 4:10–12, KJV).	"When shall he answer them, saying, Verily I say unto you, Inasmuch as ye did it not to one of the least of these, ye did it not to me. And these shall go away into everlasting punishment; but the righteous into life eternal" (Matthew 25:45–46, KJV).

CULTS
Unification Church

GODHEAD	JESUS CHRIST	HOLY SPIRIT
"Accordingly, in order to fulfill the purpose of creation, Jesus and the Holy Spirit must establish the four position foundation centered on God . . . this is called 'Trinity.'" (*Divine Principle:* Holy Spirit Association for the Unification of World Christianity, p. 217). "God either projected the full value of Himself in His object or He created nothing at all . . . So man is the visible form of God, and God is the invisible form of man. Subject and object are one in essence, God and man are one. Man is incarnate God" (*New Hope:* Sun Myung Moon, p. 5). Also see *The New Future of Christianity:* Moon, p. 28).	"Jesus, on earth, was a man no different from us except for the fact that he was without original sin" (*Divine Principle,* p. 212). "Jesus Christ is the one man who lived God's ideal in its fullest realization . . . But after his crucifixion, Christianity made Jesus into God. This is why the gap between God and man has never been bridged. Jesus is a man in whom God is incarnate. But he is not God Himself" (*New Hope,* pp.. 12–13). "Because the Jewish people disbelieved Jesus and delivered him up for crucifixion, his body was invaded by Satan, and he was killed" (*Divine Principle,* pp. 147–148).	"However, a father alone cannot give birth to children. There must be a True Mother with the True Father, in order to give rebirth to fallen children as children of goodness. She is the Holy Spirit. . . . There are many who receive revelations indicating that the Holy Spirit is a female Spirit; this is because she came as the True Mother, that is, the second Eve. Again, since the Holy Spirit is a female Spirit, we cannot become the 'bride' of Jesus unless we receive the Holy Spirit" (*Divine Principle,* p. 215).

Cults
Unification Church

SIN	SALVATION	DEATH
Since Moon's theology teaches that God is dual in essence, his doctrine of sin also is dual. There was a spiritual fall of man and a physical fall of man. "Lucifer, who felt a decrease of love, tried to tempt Eve to submit to him, in order that he might enjoy the same position in human society that he did in the angelic world. This was the motivation of the spiritual fall. . . . Eve then seduced Adam in the hope that she might rid herself of the fear derived from the fall and stand before God by becoming, even then, one body with Adam, who was meant to be her spouse. This was the motivation behind the physical fall" (*Divine Principle*, pp.. 78–80).	Man's dual nature of the fall required a dual nature in redemption, spiritual salvation and physical salvation. "If Jesus had not been crucified, what would have happened? He would have accomplished the providence of salvation both spiritually and physically" (*Divine Principle*, p. 147). "Crucifixion brought only spiritual salvation" (*New Future of Christianity*:Moon, p. 109). "God will give you your own salvation. When you become God's champion for world salvation, your own salvation is guaranteed" (*New Hope*, p. 49).	"The 'Last Days,' means the age in which hell on earth is transformed into the Kingdom of Heaven on earth" (*Divine Principle*, pp.. 111– 112). "The word of God is given by the Lord. Accepting the word brings life out of death. Such death is the hell in which we live. Thus the word of God is the Judge, and it will bring upon you a far more profound effect than the hottest flames," (*New Hope*, p. 90).

Cults

Unitarian Universalism

GODHEAD	JESUS CHRIST	HOLY SPIRIT
"Unitarians may call themselves agnostics, humanists, or even atheists. Moral values, they believe, do not require a supernatural Being for their inspiration or fulfillment" (*Introducing Unitarian Universalism:* John Nicholis Booth, p. 15). "What do Unitarians believe about God? They are free to believe whatever persuades them" (*Unitarianism, Some Questions Answered* : A. Powell Davies).	"Unitarians do not believe that Jesus is the Messiah either of Jewish hope or of Christian fantasy. They do not believe he is 'God incarnate,' or 'the Second Person in the Trinity,' or the final arbiter at the end of time who 'shall come to judge the quick and the dead'" ("What Is a Unitarian?" *Look* magazine, 3/8/55).	"Unitarians and Universalists reject the doctrine of the Trinity" (*Unitarians and Universalists Believe;* George Marshall, p. 3).

Cults
Unitarian Universalism

SIN	SALVATION	DEATH
"Unitarian Universalism is the religion of faith in man. When man sins he is blocking the perfectibility of his own conscience, for spirit is being degraded by the external act. Man is not fundamentally sinful. No man stands condemned. Given the freedom to guide himself according to the best that religion can teach, motivated by his own properly developed conscience, man can gain ultimate victory over himself" (*Introducing Unitarian Universalism*, p. 17).	"Do Unitarians believe in salvation? They believe that we have within ourselves the power of our own salvation and that reliance upon salvation through someone else's martyrdom is superstitious and contrary to the principle of moral responsibility" (*Unitarianism—Some Questions Answered*).	"A typical Unitarian statement on hell is: 'Hell is man's failure to be and live up to his best. Hell is injustice, violence, tyranny, hatred, war and everything that fits these Satanic categories. Let us go fight these evil forces here and now to help create the Paradise of which the poets speak'" (*Look*, 3/8/55, p. 80).

Cults

Rosicrucian Society of America

GODHEAD	JESUS CHRIST	HOLY SPIRIT
"We affirm the existence of One Infinite Intelligence. Omnific, Omniscient, and Omnipresent in its functions; from which we emanated as unconscious spirit substance, and to which we return as conscious, individualized entities" (*Rosicrucian Series*, S.N. 11, p. 11).	"The Son is the highest initiate of the sun period. The ordinary humanity of that period now are the archangels" (*The Rosicrucian Cosmo-Conception*, p. 376). "In studying this Trinity, first let it be clearly understood that the word 'Son' does not mean Jesus" (*Rosicrucian Fundamentals*, p. 19). "Jesus . . . had a purely natural birth, with natural parents, Mary and Joseph" (*Ibid.*, p. 151). "And note this, that while many of the 'Epistles' or writings of the Apostles speak of the 'Death of and on the Cross,' nowhere are we taught in either ancient records or the undoubtably authoritative books of the Bible itself, that Jesus actually died a physical death thereon" (*Ibid.*, p. 152).	"After the drama on Golgotha commonly called the crucifixion, the obsessing or occupying Spirit . . . was released from the physical corpus, and by entering into the earth through the blood that flowed, could thereafter send its emanations throughout the earth sphere, enfolding all humanity in its auric folds, and specially inspiring to great words and works those receptive spiritually to it . . . The aura of an evolved Spirit of Earth, he must be at least omnipresent in the sphere or domain of his jurisdiction" (*Occult Science*, Liber VI; p. 12).

Cults
Rosicrucian Society of America

SIN	SALVATION	DEATH
The Rosicrucians' theory on how man fell out of relationship with God sounds strikingly similar to the ancient heresy of Gnosticism: "From the beginning of his own existence, as a Ray of the Divine Spiritual Sun, he represented a perpendicular line, cutting in the direction of the universal will of the Source from which he emanated in the beginning. As the distance from that Source increased, and as the Ray entered into Matter, it deviated from the originally straight line and became broken, creating thereby a division of its own essence, thus establishing in matter separate will not acting in accordance with the Universal Law. (*Mercury*, Vol. 11, No 1, pp. 3–4.)	"Man, through his own individual and consciously made efforts, must attain spiritual enlightenment and ultimate immortality" (*The Secret Schools*, p. 19). "Only the good in us can deliver us from evil, or keep evil away from us" (*Rosicrucian Series*, S.N. 10, p. 6).	The Rosicrucian Society teaches universal salvation: "The final ultimate atom of the Threefold Soul, expanded into the sublime light of Cosmic Consciousness and Comprehension, will be the Force that will make of every Ego a Creative Hierarch in its due time" (*Hermetic Series*, S.N. 18, p. 3).

Cults

Mormonism

GODHEAD	JESUS CHRIST	HOLY SPIRIT
"God Himself was once as we are now, and is an exalted man, and sits enthroned in yonder heavens" (*Teachings of the Prophet Joseph Smith*, pp.. 345–347). "Many men say there is one God; the Father, the Son, the Holy Ghost are only one God. I say that is a strange God anyhow—three in one, and one is three" (*Ibid.*, p. 372). "Implicit in the Christian verity that all men are the spirit children of an Eternal Father is the usually unspoken truth that they are also the offspring of an Eternal Mother. An exalted and glorified Man of Holiness (Moses 6:57) could not be a Father unless a Woman of glory, perfection and holiness was associated with him as a Mother" (*Mormon Doctrine*: Bruce McConkie, p. 516).	In the Mormon doctrine of pre-existence, it is taught that Mother and Father God had sexual relations and produced spirit-children. The firstborn spirit-child in heaven was Jesus, known then as Jehovah; the second spirit-child was Lucifer, who became Satan. Jesus also married on earth: "It was Jesus Christ who was married, to be brought into the relation whereby he could see his seed before he was crucified" (*Journal of Discourses*, Vol. 2: Orson Hyde, p. 82). "Now, remember from this time forth, and forever, that Jesus Christ was not begotten by the Holy Ghost" (*Journal of Discourses*, Vol. 1: Brigham Young, p. 51).	"The Holy Ghost is the third member of the Godhead. He is a Personage of Spirit, a Spirit Person, a Spirit Man, a Spirit Entity. He can be in only one place at a time, and he does not and cannot transform himself into any other form or image than that of the Man whom he is, though his power and influence can be manifest at one and the same time through all immensity" (*Mormon Doctrine*, p. 359).

HANDBOOK FOR HELPING OTHERS

Cults
Mormonism

SIN	SALVATION	DEATH
"In the true gospel of Jesus Christ, there is no original sin" (*Evidences and Reconciliations*: John Widtsoe, p. 195). "The fall of man came as a blessing in disguise . . . I never speak of the part Eve took in this fall as a sin, nor do I accuse Adam of a sin . . . It is not always a sin to transgress a law. . . We can hardly look upon anything resulting.in such benefits as being a sin, in the sense in which we consider sin" (*Doctrines of Salvation*, Vol. 1: Joseph Smith, pp. 114–115).	"All men are saved by grace alone, without any act on their part, meaning they are resurrected" (*What Mormons Think of Christ*: Bruce McConkie, pp.. 24–25). "Those who gain only this general or unconditional salvation will still be judged according to their works and receive their places in a terrestrial or telestial kingdom. They will, therefore, be damned" (*Mormon Doctrine*, p. 669). "Full salvation is attained by virtue of knowledge, truth, righteousness, and all true principles. Many conditions must exist in order to make such salvations available to men. Without continuous revelation, the ministering of angels, the working of miracles, the prevalence of gifts of the spirit, there would be no salvation" (*Ibid.*, p. 670).	"Based on the eternal principle of vicarious service, the Lord has ordained Baptism for the Dead as the means whereby all his worthy children of all ages can become heirs of salvation in his kingdom" (*Mormon Doctrine*, p. 73). Note: Many of the people who have passed away are supposed to get a second chance at salvation, if they have not had a chance to hear Mormon gospel and accept it. Their live relatives will search out their genealogies and be baptized for them.

Cults

Children of God

GODHEAD	JESUS CHRIST	HOLY SPIRIT
". . . We have a Sexy God and a Sexy Religion with a Very Sexy Leader with an Extremely Sexy Young Following" (*Come On Ma!—Burn Your Bra: Moses David*, p. 2). "You'll enjoy the very wonders of total intimacy with a sexy naked God himself in a wild orgy of the Spirit as His totally surrendered Bride!" (*Ibid.*, p. 2). "Love is God!—God is Love!" (*Revolutionary Women: David*, p. 14).	"And God Himself had to have intercourse with Mother Mary in order to have Jesus" (*Revolutionary Sex*, Point 71, 3/27/73). "And this generation shall be called blessed of Me, their Father, and of David (Moses), the Shepherd . . ." (*A Psalm of David*, p. 10).	"His Holy Spirit of God is the Goddess of Love with her old Adonis, Spirit of the Love of God" (*New Nation News*, Vol. 5, No. 12, July 1973). "So if you are going to be offended at being stripped bare before God and Ravished wildly by His Spirit, how on earth are you going to stand it when He exposes your naked spirit and the spirit world in which it lives in the Letters that are yet to come? . . . A wild orgy of the Spirit . . ." (*Come On Ma!—Burn Your Bra*, pp. 1–2).

Children of God

SIN	SALVATION	DEATH
"Save your saintliness for the public! But don't be afraid to be a devilish little rascal in bed" (*Revolutionary Sex*, Point 84, 3/27/73). "For God's sake, let yourself go! Let go and let God, and enjoy the power of total surrender to the Spirit of an orgy of sexual orgasms of your God-given organs to the point that you're so wild and free in the spirit, and believe that it is so right and the way it ought to be . . ." (*Ibid.*, p. 13).	"Salvation sets us free from the curse of clothing and the shame of nakedness! We're free as Adam and Eve in the Garden before they ever sinned! If you're not, you're not fully saved" (*Come On Ma!—Burn Your Bra*, pp. 2–3). "For indeed a true Christian and a true Jew are really nothing else but Moslems, for Islam is the acceptance of the will of God, and though Mohammed was an Arab, he was God's messenger to all nations" (*Gaddaffi's Third World*, Point 46, 6/6/73).	"We were talking quietly and lovingly to one another when David's spirit helper Abrahim began to tell me of his own country through David's mouth. David would speak in Abrahim's tongue and most of what he said was in that language as Abrahim spoke through him . . ." (*Abrahim the Gypsy King!*, p. 1, 4/30/73). "Madam M: 'I think you believe in reincarnation, don't you?' David: 'In a sense. It is as though Abrahim my angelic helper comes in and blends with my body.'" (*Madam M—From One Psychic to Another!*, Point 34, p. 2, 4/25/73).

Cults

Hare Krishna

GODHEAD	JESUS CHRIST	HOLY SPIRIT
"In the beginning of the creation, there was only the Supreme Personality Narayana. There was no Brahma, no Siva, no fire, no stars in the sky, no sun. There was only Krishna who created all and enjoys all. . . . All the lists of the incarnations of Godhead are either plenary expansions of parts of the plenary expansions of the Lord, but Lord Sri Krishna is the original Personality of Godhead Himself" (*Srimad Bhagavatam*, 1:3:28).	"Jesus is the Son, and Krishna is the Father. Jesus is Krishna's Son" (*Jesus Loves Krishna*, p. 26). But is Jesus God? "Brother, why do you want to kill God? . . . You wish to 'kill' the One He loves by calling Him Jesus, the Father. But no one can end the love affair between Jesus and His Father, Krishna, by such perverted thinking"(*Ibid.*, p. 37).	To the Hare Krishnas, the Holy Spirit is the *Paramatma*: "Bhagavan, or the Personality of the Godhead, is the last word of the Absolute Truth. Paramatma is the partial representation of the Personality of the Godhead, and impersonal Brahman is the glowing effulgence of the Personality of the Godhead, as the sun rays are to the sun-god" (*Srimad Bhagavatam*, purport, 1:2:11).

Cults
Hare Krishna

SIN	SALVATION	DEATH
Sin is cleansed by personal sacrifice and discipline, eating foods sacrificed to gods, and by dancing. (See *Bhagavad-Gita, As It Is*, 4:30 and 3:13, and *The Nectar of Devotion*, p. 75).	"One should know perfectly well about the Supreme Personality of Godhead and the Transcendental Nature of his Form, Name, Abode. . . . By such Knowledge, one defeats death and enters the Kingdom of God" (*Sri Isopahishad*, Mantra 14). "God sent Jesus to be the spiritual master of a particular people in a particular place. . . . He did not claim (as others claim today) that He was the only Representative or Agent of the Supreme Person ever to walk the earth in the past or future" (*Jesus Loves Krishna*, p. 44).	"Because they are envious and mischievous, the lowest of men, I ever put them back into the ocean of material existence, into various demoniac species of life" (*Bhagavad-Gita, As It Is*, 16:19). "Those who are very sinful in their earthly life have to undergo different kinds of punishment on different planets. This punishment, however, is not eternal" (*Ibid.*, purport. 10:29).

Cults
Christian Science

GODHEAD	JESUS CHRIST	HOLY SPIRIT
"Life, Truth, and Love constitute the triune Person called God—that is, the triply divine Principle, Love. They represent a trinity in unity, three in one—the same in essence, though multiform in office: God the Father-Mother; Christ the spiritual idea of sonship; Divine Science or the Holy Comforter" (*Science and Health*: Mary Baker Eddy, pp. 331: 26–31).	"The Christian who believes in the First Commandment is a monotheist. Thus he virtually unites with the Jews' belief in one God, and recognizes that Jesus Christ is not God, as Jesus himself declared, but is the Son of God" (*Science and Health*, p. 361). "Jesus. The highest human corporeal concept of the divine idea, rebuking and destroying error and bringing to light man's immortality" (*Ibid.*, p. 589).	"Holy Ghost, Divine Science: the development of eternal Life, Truth and Love" (*Science and Health*, p. 588).

Cults
Christian Science

SIN	SALVATION	DEATH
"Here also is found . . . the cardinal point in Christian Science, that matter and evil (including all inharmony, sin, disease, death) are 'unreal'" (*Miscellaneous Writings*, p. 27).	"Man as God's idea is already saved with an everlasting salvation" (*Miscellaneous Writings*, p. 261). "The material blood of Jesus was no more efficacious to cleanse from sin when it was shed upon 'the accursed tree' than when it was flowing in his veins as he went daily about his Father's business" (*Science and Health*, p. 25, 6–9).	"Hell, Mortal belief; error; lust; remorse; hatred; revenge; sin; sickness; death; suffering and self-destruction; self-imposed agony; effects of sin; that which 'worketh abomination or maketh a lie'" (*Science and Health*, p. 588).

Cults

Baha'i

GODHEAD	JESUS CHRIST	HOLY SPIRIT
God is impersonal, and is referred to as the "Unknowable Essence." No trinity exists; rather, Baha'u'llah is God, and also the fulfillment of the Second Coming of Christ. Baha'u'llah is the promised Spirit of truth.	Jesus Christ is just one of a variety of prophets God uses to reveal Himself. Christ was the revelation for his time and age; Baha'u'llah, the founder of the Baha'i faith, is the new manifestation for this age and generation.	The Spirit of truth is Baha'u'llah.

Cults
Baha'i

SIN	SALVATION	DEATH
Imperfection and disunity are evil, and cause all of the world's problems today.	Christ's suffering is an example to show us the way to everlasting life in the spirit—just as was the suffering of other prophets. Obedience is the most important tenet of the Baha'i faith, and salvation means a reformed character, spotless deeds, and the establishment of God's Kingdom on earth.	Man must choose to follow God's latest revelation of Himself, Baha'u'llah, or he is doomed. The Baha'i faith attempts to unite all world religions; and this present age is considered the day of judgment and resurrection.

Cults

The Way

GODHEAD	JESUS CHRIST	HOLY SPIRIT
"The doctrine of the trinity states that the Father is God, the Son is God, the Holy Spirit is God, and together, not exclusively, they form one God. The trinity is co-eternal, without beginning or end, and co-equal. That defines the doctrine of the trinity, and this I do not believe the Bible teaches" (*Jesus Christ is NOT God: V. P. Wierwille*, p. 5).	It is obvious that Wierwille has confused the humanity of Christ with the Deity of Christ. The title of his book *Jesus Christ is NOT God* proclaims his theology. "They (the Father and the Son) are not 'co-eternal, without beginning or end, and co-equal'" (*Jesus Christ is NOT God*, p. 5).	The Way's theology contains two Holy Spirits. One, who is God and who is both Holy and Spirit, is spelled with a capital *S* and *H*. The other is the human holy spirit, spelled with a lower case *h* and *s*. "The Giver is God, the Spirit. . . . The gift from the Holy Spirit, the Giver, is *pneuma hagion*, holy spirit, power from on high, spiritual abilities, enablements" (*Receiving the Holy Spirit Today*: Wierwille, p. 4).

HANDBOOK FOR HELPING OTHERS

Cults
The Way

SIN	SALVATION	DEATH
"When the Natural man is born again, in what part of his being does he not commit sin? In his body and soul he still commits sin; but in that seed of God which is incorruptible, he does not commit sin" (*Power for Abundant Living*: Wierwille, p. 292).	"The moment a person confesses with his mouth Jesus as Lord, that person is converted, saved, born again. . . . Confess with thy mouth does not say confess one's sins. If it had said 'confess your sins,' salvation would be of works; and we are not saved by works, but by grace" (*Power for Abundant Living*, pp. 296-298).	"Many Christians hold the belief that upon death those who belong to Christ are immediately received up into glory, commonly called Heaven or paradise, to appear before the Father. There they are alive and conscious and have a joyous existence with Him and their loved ones. Such a belief is contrary to the teachings in the Word of God . . . . The Biblical description of gravedom . . . is a place where there is no consciousness and thus no remembrance" (*Are the Dead Alive Now?*: Wierwille, pp. 21–23). Note: This doctrine is commonly called "soul-sleep" because the participants believe they will sleep until the Resurrection.

Cults
Scientology

GODHEAD	JESUS CHRIST	HOLY SPIRIT
"The curse of the past has been a pretense of knowledge. We've had a worship of the fable. We have had prayers being sent up to myth" (*Scientology: A New Slant on Life*: L. Ron Hubbard, p. 52). "The Supreme Being is Survive. The Devil is Succumb" (*Science of Survival, Book II*, p. 31).	"Another basic concept Scientology shares with universal religious thought is reincarnation. . . . It is believed by many authorities that Jesus was a member of the cult of the Essenes, who believed in reincarnation . . ." (*Scientology: A World Religion Emerges in the Space Age*: Church of Scientology Information Service, 1974, p. 15). "Neither Lord Buddha nor Jesus Christ were OT's [Operating Thetan, highest state there is], according to evidence. They were just a shade above clear" (*Certainty* magazine, Vol. 5, No. 10, Hubbard).	No mention.

Cults
Scientology

SIN	SALVATION	DEATH
"Axiom 31, Goodness and badness, beautifulness and ugliness, are alike considerations and have no other basis than 'Opinion'" (*Scientology 0–8*: Hubbard, p. 33). "Good is being more right than one is wrong. . . . Evil is the opposite of good, and is anything which is destructive more than it is constructive along any of the various dynamics . . . Good, bluntly, is survival. Evil is non-survival" (*Science of Survival*: Hubbard, pp. 33–34).	Before one can "know the Supreme Being," he has to have his "engrams" and "overts" (sins) removed through an Auditor rather than by Jesus Christ's atonement. "Personal salvation in one's lifetime [is] freedom from the cycle of birth and death [reincarnation]. . . . Religious practice of all Faiths is the universal way to Wisdom, Understanding and/or salvation" (*Scientology, a World Religion*, pp. 16, 35).	"And you don't have to go to Heaven or to Hell if you don't want to. . . . And you can be immortal and yet have your body" (*The Golden Dawn*: Hubbard, 1972). "Hell is a total myth, an invention just to make people very unhappy, and is a vicious lie" (*Professional Auditor's Bulletin #130*, Hubbard).

Cults
Jehovah's Witnesses

GODHEAD	JESUS CHRIST	HOLY SPIRIT
"Satan is the originator of the 'trinity' doctrine" (*Let God Be True*, p. 82). "The Bible shows that there is only one God, the Most High, the Almighty. . . . That the Father is greater and older than the Son is reasonable, easy to understand and is what the Bible teaches" (*From Paradise Lost to Paradise Regained*, p. 164).	"The Word or Logos is not God or the God, but is the Son of God, and hence is a god" (*New World Translation*, p. 775). "The very fact that he was sent proves he was not equal with God but was less than God the Father" (*The Word: Who is He? According to John*, p. 19). "Scriptural evidence indicates that the name Michael applied to God's Son before he left heaven to become Jesus Christ and also after his return . . . Michael is actually the Son of God" (*Aid to Bible Understanding*, p. 1152). "The man Jesus is dead, forever dead" (*Studies in the Scriptures*, Vol. V, p. 454).	"Far from teaching equality with Jehovah, the Scriptures show that the holy spirit is not even a person. . . . God's holy spirit is not a God, not a member of a trinity, not co-equal, and is not even a person. . . . It is God's active force, not Jehovah's power residing within himself, but his energy when projected out from himself. . . . It is not a blind, uncontrolled force, such as the forces of 'nature,' lightning, hurricanes and the like, but . . . is at all times under his control . . . and therefore may be likened to a radar beam" (*The Watchtower*, 7/15/57, pp. 431-433).

Cults

Jehovah's Witnesses

SIN	SALVATION	DEATH
"There are two kinds of sin, Scripturally speaking: 1. Inherited, which 'does not incur death,' i.e., from which there is hope of being released; 2. Willful, which brings a sentence of everlasting destruction" (*Make Sure of All Things*, pp. 344). "The Bible clearly teaches that the dead are unconscious and lifeless in the grave" (*The Truth that Leads to Eternal Life*, p. 34).	"You must love Jehovah's universal sovereignty just as his Son Jesus Christ does; you must uphold it and proclaim it and remain true to it at all costs until it is vindicated. Only then may you survive Armageddon" (*You May Survive Armageddon into God's New World*, p. 39). "The justice of God would not permit that Jesus, as a ransom, be more than a perfect man; and certainly not be the supreme God Almighty in the flesh" (*Let God Be True*, p. 87). "So from among mankind only 144,000 persons will ever go to Heaven" (*From Paradise Lost to Paradise Regained*, p. 186).	"False religion teaches that hell is a place where the wicked suffer. . . . This unreasonable doctrine contradicts the Bible" (*Make Sure of All Things*, pp. 154–155). "Who is responsible for this God-dishonoring doctrine? The promulgator of it is Satan himself" (*Let God Be True*, p. 79).

Cults

Theosophy

GODHEAD	JESUS CHRIST	HOLY SPIRIT
"In divine essence, latent power and potential spirituality, man is an image of God, because he is part of Him" (*Elementary Theosophy*, p. 23).	"All men are innate divinity . . . so in time all men become christs. (*Is Theosophy Anti-Christian?*: Annie Besant, p. 16).	No mention.

Cults
Theosophy

SIN	SALVATION	DEATH
"The hypothesis of reincarnation shows our inherent divinity, and the method by which the latent becomes the actual. Instead of the ignoble belief that we can fling our sins upon another, it makes personal responsibility the keynote of life" (*Elementary Theosophy*, p. 206).	"It is the pernicious doctrine that wrongdoing by one can be set right by the sacrifice of another" (*Elementary Theosophy*, pp. 201–6).	"The idea of a hot hell is an afterthought, the distortion of an astronomical allegory" (*Theosophical Glossary:* H. P. Blavatsky, p. 139).

Cults
Armstrongism

GODHEAD	JESUS CHRIST	HOLY SPIRIT
"I suppose most people think of God as one single individual person. Or, as a 'trinity.' This is not true. . . . But the theologians and 'Higher Critics' have blindly accepted the heretical and false doctrine introduced by pagan false prophets who crept in, that the Holy Spirit is a third person—the heresy of the 'trinity.' This limits God to 'Three Persons.' This denies that Christ, through His Holy Spirit, actually comes now into the converted Christian and does His saving work on the inside" (*Just What Do You Mean—Born Again?* Herbert W. Armstrong, pp. 17–19).	God becomes man, saved: "But He was not God inside of, yet separate from the body of flesh—He, God, was made of flesh, until He, still God—God, with us—God in (not inside of) the human flesh—God manifest in the flesh (1 Timothy 3:16)" (*The Plain Truth,* April 1963, p. 10). "Jesus, alone of all humans, has so far been saved! By the resurrective power of God! When Jesus comes, at the time of the resurrection of those in Christ, He then brings His reward with Him!" (*Why Were You Born?,* Armstrong, p. 11).	"The Holy Spirit is not a person. . . . The Holy Spirit is not the third member of the Godhead" (*Is God a Trinity?*: George Johnson, pp. 37–39). "One thing more, the Holy Spirit is divine, spiritual love—the love of God flowing into you from God Almighty—through the living Christ!" (*What Do You Mean . . . Salvation?,* Armstrong, p. 23).

HANDBOOK FOR HELPING OTHERS

Cults
Armstrongism

SIN	SALVATION	DEATH
God is responsible for man's sin: "God has made man's natural mind so that it wants to do things that are contrary to His laws. . . . God, in love and wisdom, blinds human beings who by nature reject the truth so they will unwittingly sin all the more often and thereby learn their lesson all the more deeply" (*Is This the Only Day of Salvation?*: C. P. Meredith, p. 2).	"People have been taught, falsely, that 'Christ completed the plan of salvation on the Cross.' . . . The popular denominations have taught, 'Just believe—that's all there is to it; believe on the Lord Jesus Christ, and you are that instant saved!' That teaching is false. . . . The blood of Christ does not finally save any man . . ." (*All About Water Baptism*, p. 2).	"But Jesus did not describe a place where the wicked are tortured forever and ever. . . . The wicked will be consumed, and their remains will be just the ashes and vapours left from the fire that burns them up. They will be dead, for all eternity" (*Lazarus and the Rich Man*: Armstrong, p. 6). "When God punishes the wicked the fire will be unquenchable! But that doesn't say it won't burn itself out when it has nothing more to burn. . . . That is the end of the wicked! They shall perish and not be any more (*Ibid*., p. 14).

Chapter 32

SORCERY AND THE OCCULT

In his search for the purpose of life, man must choose whom he will serve: God, or that which is not God. Some try to find their answers outside the Bible, often through spiritism and the occult, which originate with Satan and lead only to destruction.

32.1 GOD'S WARNINGS

How should we counsel those deceived by the adversary so that they will recognize their sin, repent, and be released through the Lord Jesus Christ? First, what does the Bible say about sorcery and the occult?

"But realize this, that in the last days difficult times will come. For men will be lovers of self, lovers of money, boastful, arrogant, revilers, disobedient to parents, ungrateful, unholy, unloving, irreconcilable, malicious gossips, without self-control, brutal, haters of good, treacherous, reckless, conceited, lovers of pleasure rather than lovers of God; holding to a form of godliness, although they have denied its power; and avoid such men as these" (2 Timothy 3:1–5).

The problems begin when men love self more than God, when they choose their own way over God's.

Further, the apostle Paul wrote,

"Now I urge you, brethren, keep your eye on those who cause dissensions and hindrances contrary to the teaching which you learned, and turn away from them. For such men are slaves not of our Lord Christ but of their own appetites; and by their smooth and flattering speech they deceive the hearts of the unsuspecting. For the report of your obedience has reached to all; therefore I am rejoicing over you, but I want you to be wise in what is good, and innocent in what is evil. And the God of peace will soon crush Satan under your feet" (Romans 16:17–20).

We do not need to go into an in-depth study of the occult or cults. But the following material will provide a broad overview and some keys to the subject.

We might first make a comparison with how the U.S. Treasury Department determines if a bill is counterfeit. Have they studied many counterfeits? No. They have studied the real thing, and can therefore determine what is counterfeit. We study God's Word, the Bible, and therefore reject anything that does not line up with that.

The Bible exhorts us: "Any one who goes too far and does not abide in the teaching of Christ, does not have God; the one who abides in the teaching, he has both the Father and the Son. If any one comes to you and does not bring this teaching, do not receive him into your house, and do not give him a greeting; for the one who gives him a greeting participates in his evil deeds" (2 John 9–11; see also Deuteronomy 12:29–30; Matthew 24:24; 2 Thessalonians 2:8–9; 1 Timothy 4:1; Revelation 16:14.)

While the enemy tries to deceive us or those we

counsel, and put us under bondage to deception and the powers of darkness, we can be set free by knowing Jesus Christ and His power within us. "If therefore the Son shall make you free, you shall be free indeed" (John 8:36).

God's Word forbids sorcery of any kind in Deuteronomy 18:9–14, an important passage of Scripture:

"When you enter the land which the Lord your God gives you, you shall not learn to imitate the detestable things of those nations. There shall not be found among you anyone who makes his son or his daughter pass through the fire, one who uses divination, one who practices witchcraft, or one who interprets omens, or a sorcerer, or one who casts a spell, or a medium, or a spiritist, or one who calls up the dead. For whoever does these things is detestable to the Lord; and because of these detestable things the Lord your God will drive them out before you. You shall be blameless before the Lord your God. For those nations, which you shall dispossess, listen to those who practice witchcraft and to diviners, but as for you, the Lord your God has not allowed you to do so." (See also Leviticus 19:26–28, 31.)

We who are in the light have *no* justification for using the tools of darkness. Our source is the Light of the world, Jesus Christ. We do not turn to those practices that God denounces. (See Malachi 3:5 and Isaiah 8:19.)

32.2 DEFINITIONS

The following definitions will help us recognize those practices that God forbids.

Divination (Soothsayer, augur, seer): discovering what is obscure or foretelling future events as by supernatural means.

Sorcery (wizardry): the art, practices, or spells of a sorcerer; magic, ESP, black magic, in which supernatural powers are exercised through the aid of evil spirits; witchery.

Occult: beyond the bounds of ordinary knowledge; mysterious.

Necromancy: magic in general; enchantment; conjuration; the pretended art of divination through communication with the dead; black art.

Magicians: those who practice the art or science of influencing or controlling the course of nature, events, and supernatural powers through occult science or mysterious arts; includes necromancy, exorcism, dreams, shaking arrows, astrology, soothsaying, divining rods, witchcraft.

32.3 GOD'S JUDGMENTS

The Bible says God will pass judgment on those who delve into sorcery and the occult. Deception will cease. "Women will no longer see false visions or practice divination" and God will deliver His people out of the hand of those who do (see Ezekiel 13:23; see also Ezekiel 12:23–24 and Micah 5:12–15).

Magicians will be confounded: "I, the Lord, am the maker of all things . . . Causing the omens of boasters to fail, Making fools out of diviners, Causing wise men to draw back, And turning their knowledge into foolishness" (Isaiah 44:24–25; see also Daniel 2:27; 4:7; 5:7–8; Micah 3:7).

God will never close His eyes to the practice of the occult. He punishes disobedience, just as He did in the case of Saul: "So Saul died for his trespass which he committed against the Lord, because of the word of the Lord which he did not keep; and also because he asked counsel of a medium, making inquiry of it, and did not inquire of the Lord. Therefore He killed him, and turned the kingdom to David the son of Jesse" (1 Chronicles 10:13–14).

Sorcerers, along with the cowardly, the unbelieving, the abominable, murderers, immoral people, idolaters, and liars, will have their part "in the lake that burns with fire and brimstone, which is the second death" (see Revelation 21:8; see also Exodus 22:18; Deuteronomy 13:5; 1 Samuel 28:7–25; Isaiah 47:9–15; 57:3–13; Malachi 3:5; Acts 19:19; Revelation 22:15).

32.4 DANGER ZONES

God's Word forbids Christians to take part in all doctrines and practices of darkness. Some are listed here.

Mind Science. The false teaching that mind is the only reality, and that matter, sickness, and sin are not real, just error. Christian Science is one such group.

Reincarnation: Karma (Hinduism and Buddhism). The false belief that a person dies and his soul returns in another body or form.

The Bible says, "Inasmuch as it is appointed for men to die once, and after this comes judgment" (Hebrews 9:27; see also Luke 16:20–31 and Revelation 20:5).

Denial of the Trinity, the deity of Jesus Christ, His bodily resurrection, or His Second Coming.

Eclecticism. Acceptance of good in all religions; still searching for truth; not acknowledging that Christianity is founded on the person of Jesus Christ and not just on His teachings.

Jesus said to him, "I am the way, and the truth, and the life; no one comes to the Father, but through Me" (John 14:6). There is only one God and one way to Him—Jesus Christ. (See Matthew 7:13–14.)

Metaphysics. Confusing soul and spirit; trying to contact God with the mind instead of the spirit.

Precognition or fortune-telling. "Dead" or fixed fate, laid out, unchangeable, by visions, crystal ball, tarot cards, tea leaves, palm reading, ouija board or planchette, graphology.

We are not to look to any other source than God to discover our futures. We must not open ourselves or our children to any of these demonic influences. We do not need anyone or anything but God and His wisdom.

Extrasensory Perception. Telepathy, clairvoyance, mind-reading, diagnosis of disease and prescription of cures by clairvoyance, water-witching (or dowsing), pendulum or divining rod usage.

Astrology. Horoscopes (worship of the hosts of heaven).

Stars can be signs but cannot have power to influence human lives. It is estimated that fifteen percent of all Americans run their lives by astrology. But we do not need to look to the stars. We look only to God who holds our future.

"You are wearied with your many counsels; Let now the astrologers, Those who prophesy by the stars, Those who predict by the new moons, Stand up and save you from what will come upon you. Behold, they have become like stubble, Fire burns them; They cannot deliver themselves from the power of the flame; There will be no coal to warm by; Nor a fire to sit before!" (Isaiah 47:13–14).

Mind Expansion. Techniques including drugs, hypnosis, transcendental meditation, third eye, self-hypnotism, metaphysical healing of the body.

Sorcery or Witchcraft. Hexing, influencing or harassing others by psychic and occult means, magic, sleight of hand, ventriloquism, charms, potions, amulets (objects worn to ward off evil or "protecting" charms), hexes, control of others by mental suggestion.

Physical Phenomena. Telekinesis (attempts to control movement of matter by thought), levitation, table-tipping (attempts to neutralize gravity by psychic means), automatic writing, psychic surgery, diagnosis by wooden rod, and treatment by color.

Spiritism or Spiritualism. Seances, contact with the spirit world, departed relatives, and friends through spirit guides and mediums (not dreams or visions, but alleged return of the departed to this world).

Satan Worship. Secret societies, blood pacts.

Hypnotism. Some Christians use hypnosis in different forms, but the Bible says, "There shall not be found among you . . . one who casts a spell, or a medium, or a spiritist, or one who calls up the dead" (Deuteronomy 18:10–11; see also Isaiah 19:3).

32.5 ESCAPE FROM THE OCCULT

How do we counsel those who have been involved in occult practices?

We need, first of all, to listen to what they say to determine what their problem is. Preaching will not help but sharing God's love will.

We should help them realize that occult involvement is sin, according to the Bible, and that the Lord Jesus Christ wants to release them from the power such involvement has had over their lives. They must confess and repent of their sinful involvement and renounce their past activities. This includes burning or destroying *all* symbols of *any* occult practice (see Acts 19:19), and in some cases it includes deliverance. (See Chapter 33, Deliverance.)

We should encourage them to attend a church where they will receive sound biblical teaching and fellowship with other Christians as they grow toward spiritual maturity.

One final word: We should study the good, the truth of God's Word, so that we will become wise in that which is good and innocent in that which is evil (see Romans 16:19). In looking to the Light, we will escape the darkness.

Chapter 33

DELIVERANCE

Deliverance includes being set free from sin and from demonic influence or oppression. In counseling those who may need deliverance, we must ask for wisdom and guidance from the Holy Spirit to discern the true nature of the problem.

Most Christians do not have experience in deliverance or in confronting demonic spirits. For this reason, unless God directs otherwise, it is wise to refer someone who needs deliverance to one or more persons who can provide counsel and help.

In the closing verses of Matthew's Gospel, Jesus said that all authority had been given to Him "in heaven and on earth" and that He would be with us always. (See Matthew 28:18–20.) Because of His Spirit dwelling inside us, we have that same authority in heaven and on earth that God has given us over the enemy.

Many people use demons as an excuse not to confront sin. They look for a demon behind every tree or under every chair, blaming the enemy for every crisis, ache, or trial. But often it is their failure to resolve sin—resentment, bitterness, unforgiveness, and the like—that has resulted in that crisis, ache, or trial. Sin blocks the work of God's Spirit. If sin is the problem rather than spiritual oppression, we need to lead the person to confession and repentance, that he might be released from the power sin has over his life.

33.1 CAN CHRISTIANS HAVE DEMONS?

When a person receives Jesus Christ into his life as Lord and Savior, the Holy Spirit comes in and seals his spirit (see Ephesians 1:13). He cannot, therefore, in my opinion, be influenced (controlled) by demonic spirits.

Satan has no freedom to act in a life without God's permission. God allowed Satan to touch Job's life and test him, as we have already seen; otherwise Satan could not have done do. (See Job 1:6–12.) Jesus even had to give the demons permission to enter the swine (see Mark 5:12–13; also Luke 22:31–32).

Someone whose life is filled with the Lord Jesus has no room for evil, for how can darkness be put into something full of light? Furthermore, Jesus did not come to destroy Himself when He takes up residence in a person's life. "The Son of God appeared for this purpose, that He might destroy the works of the devil" (1 John 3:8).

So Christians who are filled with the Holy Spirit and walking by God's principles, as I read the Scriptures, cannot entertain demons. But a person who has come out of a deep background in witchcraft may have some residual activity. The majority of us who have never lived in that realm of darkness would not tolerate demonic spirits.

We all have times of spiritual oppression, when the enemy shoots his fiery darts and seeks to devour us. But that is not being under demonic control. We simply exercise our God-given authority over the enemy and command him to leave in Jesus name.

33.2 GUIDELINES FOR DELIVERANCE

The following guidelines and Scriptures will help us as we counsel in deliverance.

First, we are in a spiritual battle.

"For our struggle is not against flesh and blood, but against the rulers, against the powers, against the world forces of this darkness, against the spiritual forces of wickedness in the heavenly places" (Ephesians 6:12; see also 1 Chronicles 21:1; 2 Corinthians 2:11; 10:3–5; 1 Peter 5:8).

Then we prepare for battle. We put on our spiritual weapons and leave them on at all times. Even at night as we sleep, we need our spiritual armor on to protect us from the enemy's attacks.

"Finally, be strong in the Lord, and in the strength of His might. Put on the full armor of God, that you may be able to stand firm against the schemes of the devil. Therefore, take up the full armor of God, that you may be able to resist in the evil day, and having done everything, to stand firm. Stand firm therefore, having girded your loins with truth, and having put on the breastplate of righteousness, and having shod your feet with the preparation of the gospel of peace; in addition to all, taking up the shield of faith with which you will be able to extinguish all the flaming missiles of the evil one. And take the helmet of salvation, and the sword of the Spirit, which is the word of God. With all prayer and petition pray at all times in the Spirit" (Ephesians 6:10–11, 13–18a).

Clothed in the whole armor of God, we fight the battle by:

Resistance. "Submit therefore to God. Resist the devil and he will flee from you" (James 4:7). The key to resisting the enemy is submitting to God first. That means focusing on the Lord Jesus, looking at Him and not at the forces of darkness and Satan. Then the enemy will flee.

Faith. The enemy is defeated by our faith in God. "Simon, Simon, behold, Satan has demanded permission to sift you like wheat; but I have prayed for you, that your faith may not fail; and you, when once you have turned again, strengthen your brothers" (Luke 22:31; see also Matthew 17:20–21).

The Blood of Jesus. "And they overcame him because of the blood of the Lamb and because of the word of their testimony, and they did not love their life even to death" (Revelation 12:11).

Walking in the Spirit. "But I say, walk by the Spirit, and you will not carry out the desire of the flesh. For the flesh sets its desire against the Spirit, and the Spirit against the flesh; for these are in opposition to one another, so that you may not do the things that you please" (Galatians 5:16–17).

Divine Power. We must take authority over every lustful, sinful, negative thought. If it does not agree with God's Word, we reject it.

"For though we walk in the flesh, we do not war according to the flesh, for the weapons of our warfare are not of the flesh, but divinely powerful for the destruction of fortresses. We are destroying speculations and every lofty thing raised up against the knowledge of God, and we are taking every thought captive to the obedience of Christ" (2 Corinthians 10:3–5).

Worship. When Satan tempted Jesus in the wilderness to worship him, Jesus answered him, "It is written, 'You shall worship the Lord your God and serve Him only'" (Luke 4:8). Our worship of God routs the enemy because he hates God and hates for us to worship Him.

Praise. "Yet Thou art holy, O Thou who are enthroned upon the praises of Israel" (Psalm 22:3). God lives in our praises, making it impossible for the enemy to be present. Darkness cannot enter light, for light puts out the darkness.

Prayer and Fasting. Jesus' disciples asked Him why they could not cast out an unclean spirit from a boy. He answered them, "This kind cannot come out by anything but prayer"—and many manuscripts add, "and fasting" (Mark 9:29).

Authority. The enemy knows Jesus has given us authority over him. Jesus told His disciples, "These signs will accompany those who have believed: in My name they will cast out demons" (Mark 16:17; see also Matthew 10:1; Mark 3:13–15; 6:7; Luke 10:17–20; 9:1–2).

A person needs deliverance when sin dominates his life. In Jesus' words:

"That which proceeds out of the man, that is what defiles the man. For from within, out of the heart of men, proceed the evil thoughts and fornications, thefts, murders, adulteries, deeds of coveting and wickedness, as well as deceit, sensuality, envy, slander, pride and foolishness. All these evil things proceed from within and defile the man" (Mark 7:20–23).

A person must take specific steps before he can be set free from sin or demonic influence:

He must humble himself before God.

He needs to be honest, and confess and repent of his sin and any contact with evil spirits.

He needs to ask forgiveness of all persons involved and request the counselor's specific prayer for forgiveness.

He must surrender completely to the Lordship of Christ, asking Him to take charge of his life.

33.3 RECEIVING DELIVERANCE

If the need stems from the sin of the lust of the flesh, then a person must daily, methodically give up those desires of the flesh. "Now those who belong to Christ Jesus have crucified the flesh with its passions and desires" (Galatians 5:24; see also Romans 6; Galatians 2:20; Revelation 12:11).

At the same time, we must bind or restrict the adversary from working in our lives. "Truly I say to you, whatever you shall bind on earth shall have been bound in heaven; and whatever you loose on earth shall have been loosed in heaven" (Matthew 18:18; see also Matthew 12:29; 16:19; Luke 11:21–22).

We speak the word to the enemy, for Satan has to obey Jesus. "And the demons began to entreat [Jesus], saying, 'If you are going to cast us out, send us into the herd of swine.' And He said to them, 'Begone!' And they came out, and went into the swine, and behold, the whole herd rushed down the steep bank into the sea and perished in the waters" (Matthew 8:31–32; see also Mark 1:23–26; 5:1–13; 9:25–27; Luke 8:30–33).

We ask God to deliver the person and believe that He will. God alone delivers. "For it is He who delivers you from the snare of the trapper" (Psalm 91:3).

And the one whom God sets free "shall be free indeed" (see John 8:36).

There are a number of helpful principles to keep in mind: First, do not converse with the adversary. Second, do not pray long deliverance prayers. God answers short prayers as effectively as long ones. (See Ecclesiastes 5:1–3; Psalm 119:11; Matthew 4:4; Ephesians 6:17.) Third, do not get loud. God hears the soft voice of a child who speaks only the powerful name of Jesus. And fourth, do not get impressed with deliverance. It is the name of Jesus that causes evil spirits to leave, not our counsel.

Do, on the other hand . . .

Confess the Word. " 'The word is near you, in your mouth and in your heart'—that is, the word of faith which we are preaching, that if you confess with your mouth Jesus as Lord, and believe in your heart that God raised Him from the dead, you shall be saved" (Romans 10:8–9; see also Hebrews 3:1; Revelation 12:11).

Cultivate Right Relationships. One must separate himself from those relationships and surroundings that were part of the former way of living. "Therefore, do not be partakers with them; for you were formerly darkness, but now you are light in the Lord; walk as children of light" (Ephesians 5:7–8).

Paul also said, "I also do my best to maintain always a blameless conscience both before God and before men" (Acts 24:16; see also 2 Corinthians 6:14).

Make Jesus Lord. "Now judgment is upon this world; now the ruler of this world shall be cast out. And I, if I be lifted up from the earth, will draw all men to Myself" (John 12:31–32).

Fellowship with Other Believers. We are not to forsake "our own assembling together, as some do, but we are to gather and encourage one another" (see Hebrews 10:25).

Pray Constantly. Paul tells us to "pray without ceasing" (1 Thessalonians 5:17).

33.4 STAYING FREE

To remain free from sin and demonic influence or oppression, we must:

Yield to the Lord. "Now do not stiffen your neck like your fathers, but yield to the Lord and enter His sanctuary which He has consecrated forever, and serve the Lord your God, that His burning anger may turn away from you" (2 Chronicles 30:8).

Be Filled with the Spirit. "Do not get drunk with wine, for that is dissipation, but be filled with the Spirit, speaking to one another in psalms and hymns and spiritual songs, singing and making melody with your heart to the Lord" (Ephesians 5:18–19).

We are to be filled with the Spirit out of obedience to God (see Ephesians 5:17) and to protect ourselves from evil. And once a person has received deliverance, he must be filled with the Holy Spirit to keep all other spirits out. (See Luke 11:24–26.)

Study the Word. The apostle Paul wrote to Timothy, "Be diligent to present yourself approved to God as a workman who does not need to be ashamed, handling accurately the word of truth" (2 Timothy 2:15).

All of these are necessary to maintain a life free from the power of sin and darkness.

Closing Statement

You have just completed chapters of practical and biblical insights into God's Word.

From this point on, what you do with this knowledge—how you apply it in your life and the lives of others—is up to you.

May you accept that challenge to take what you have learned and put it to work in your own life. Then you will find power in sharing it with others, that many might be set free and "mount up with wings like eagles" (see Isaiah 40:31) to the glory and honor of our Lord.